BIOGRAPHY:

Arlind, an extraordinary entrepreneur born in Macedonia, emerges as a dynamic force with a rich tapestry of experience spanning various industries. Growing up in a small Eastern European town, Arlind ignited his passion for business at a young age, perpetually seeking avenues to create value and contribute to others' success.

Embarking on his entrepreneurial journey in the USA, Arlind founded Prestige Productions in his early twenties, offering event planning and management services to the Entertainment industry. Fueled by his innate marketing talent and unwavering drive for success, Arlind swiftly established a stellar reputation for delivering exceptional service and curating unforgettable events.

Venturing into larger horizons, Arlind co-founded International Events LLC, specialising in organising large-scale events and conferences. Simultaneously, he played a pivotal role in the establishment of Impact LLC and Impact Marketing, providing invaluable marketing and branding services across diverse industries.Arlind's fascination with technology led him to co-found Lunar Solutions, a cutting-edge software development company serving clients in various industries. His entrepreneurial spirit extended to Aurora Consulting Group, offering strategic consulting services to empower businesses in their growth and success endeavours. In 2008 driven by a love for hospitality, Arlind co-founded Restaurant Investment Group, introducing successful restaurant concepts across multiple U.S. cities, including Chicago, Scottsdale, and Dallas.

The company's unwavering focus on exceptional customer service and unique dining experiences swiftly garnered a loyal customer base, propelling it to a leadership position in the industry.In 2019, Arlind founded Impact Global Networks, a consulting firm at the intersection of wealth strategy, marketing, hospitality, IT, and blockchain technology. With a talented team, Arlind has been instrumental in guiding numerous clients toward success and facilitating the growth of their businesses.

Throughout his illustrious career, Arlind has proven to be a visionary entrepreneur, continually seeking innovative ways to create value and foster success for others. His unique strategic approach, combined with an unwavering passion for success and dedication to clients, has rightfully positioned him as a leader in the business world.Arlind's success can be attributed to his exceptional ability to adapt to changing market conditions and trends, coupled with an innovative problem-solving approach. A true pioneer in the cryptocurrency and blockchain industry, he has played a pivotal role in driving the global adoption of these transformative technologies.

Beyond entrepreneurship, Arlind's expertise in wealth strategy has been a beacon for his clients, guiding them to financial success through innovative investment strategies. His commitment to building long-term relationships, marked by personal attention to detail, has been a cornerstone of his success. As a multifaceted entrepreneur and innovator, Arlind has earned recognition as a true leader in his field. Numerous awards and invitations to speak at global conferences underscore his significant contributions to entrepreneurship, marketing, and blockchain technology.

Arlind's ability to co-found multiple successful companies across diverse industries showcases a unique perspective and deep understanding of business dynamics. His leadership skills, characterised by motivation and inspiration, have propelled his companies to rapid growth and leadership positions in their respective industries.Despite a demanding schedule, Arlind remains devoted to giving back to the community, actively participating in charitable organizations and supporting the education and development of young entrepreneurs. In addition to his established ventures, Arlind recently co-founded SkenderPay, a groundbreaking cryptocurrency built on AI and blockchain technology, garnering significant interest from global investors and businesses. SkenderPay, created in response to the growing demand for a secure and decentralized transaction system, reflects Arlind's vision to leverage blockchain technology for innovative solutions. His tireless efforts have resulted in a platform that not only prioritizes security and efficiency but is also user-friendly and accessible to a diverse audience. Recognized and well-received by the cryptocurrency community, SkenderPay stands as a testament to Arlind's deep understanding of the industry, coupled with his prowess in marketing and entrepreneurship. As an innovative entrepreneur and pioneer in the cryptocurrency realm, Arlind's co-founding of SkenderPay underscores his commitment to developing cutting-edge solutions that meet the evolving needs of businesses and individuals.

In his leisure time, Arlind indulges his love for travel, exploring diverse cultures, and remains an avid reader, constantly seeking new knowledge to stay abreast of the latest trends in business and technology.

Arlind Sadiku

Impact Global Network

Founder & CEO

The first degree of success is setting goals.

"The more specific and measurable your goal, the more likely you are to achieve it."

This means having a clear idea of what you want to accomplish and working towards achieving those goals. It is important to set both short-term and long-term goals, as this will help you stay focused and motivated. Setting goals is an essential part of achieving success in any area of your life. Whether you want to improve your health, advance in your career, or simply enjoy more fulfilment and happiness, setting goals can help you get there. Some benefits of setting goals and objectives include:

Clarity: Goals and objectives provide a clear sense of direction and focus, helping you to determine what is most important and prioritise your time and efforts.
Motivation: Having specific goals and objectives can help to motivate and inspire you to take action and make progress towards achieving them.
Measurement: Setting goals and objectives allows you to track your progress and measure your success, helping you to see how far you have come and where you need to go next.
Accountability: Sharing your goals and objectives with others can help to hold you accountable for making progress towards achieving them.

Overall, setting goals and objectives can help you to stay focused, motivated, and on track as you work towards achieving your desired outcomes

You might ask yourself, but how do you set goals that will actually lead to success? Here are some key steps to follow and start with:

Identify your values and priorities. What matters most to you in life? What do you want to achieve, and why is it important to you? Answering these questions will help you focus on the goals that align with your values and priorities. Be specific and measurable. Instead of setting a vague goal like "I want to be healthy," set a specific and measurable goal like "I want to lose 20 pounds by June 1st." This will make it easier to track your progress and know when you've reached your goal. Make your goals challenging but achievable. Your goals should push you out of your comfort zone, but they should also be realistic. If your goal is too easy, you won't feel motivated to pursue it. If it's too difficult, you may become discouraged and give up.

Break your goals down into smaller, actionable steps. Instead of trying to tackle your goal all at once, break it down into smaller, more manageable steps. For example, if your goal is to save $10,000 for a down payment on a house, you could break it down into monthly savings targets or set up automatic transfers to your savings account.

Create a plan and schedule for achieving your goals. Once you've identified your goals and broken them down into actionable steps, create a plan and schedule for achieving them. This will help you stay on track and make progress towards your goals.

Stay accountable and track your progress. It's important to regularly check in on your progress and make adjustments to your plan as needed. You can do this by setting up regular check-ins with a friend or accountability partner, or by keeping a journal to track your progress. By following these steps and staying committed to your goals, you can set yourself up for success in any area of your life. Remember to celebrate your successes along the way, and don't be afraid to reassess and adjust your goals as needed. With focus and determination, you can achieve anything you set your mind to.As you work towards achieving your goals, remember to be patient and persistent. Success rarely happens overnight, and it's important to stay focused and committed, even when you face challenges or setbacks.One way to stay motivated and on track is to regularly remind yourself why your goals are important to you. This can help you stay focused on the bigger picture and keep your eyes on the prize.

Another tip is to seek out support and guidance from others. Whether it's a mentor, a coach, or a supportive friend or family member, having someone in your corner can provide valuable advice and encouragement as you work towards your goals.

Finally, remember to be flexible and adaptable. Life is unpredictable, and you may need to adjust your goals or your plan as you go. Don't be afraid to reassess and make changes as needed, but also don't give up on your goals just because things don't go exactly as you planned.

By following these tips and staying committed to your goals, you can achieve success and reach new heights in any area of your life. Remember to celebrate your successes along the way, and keep pushing forward towards your goals. With focus and determination, you can accomplish anything you set your mind to. In addition to setting goals and working towards them, it's also important to maintain a positive attitude and mindset. This can be especially important when you face challenges or setbacks. One way to stay positive is to focus on the progress you're making, rather than getting bogged down by obstacles or setbacks. Celebrate your small victories and milestones along the way, and remind yourself of how far you've come. Another way to maintain a positive attitude is to surround yourself with supportive and encouraging people.

This can include friends, family, colleagues, or mentors who can offer encouragement and guidance. It's also helpful to practise gratitude and focus on the things you're grateful for. When you're feeling down or frustrated, take a moment to reflect on the good things in your life and remind yourself of all the things you have to be thankful for. Finally, remember to take care of yourself and prioritise your wellbeing. This can include things like getting enough sleep, eating well, and exercising regularly. When you're feeling your best, you'll be better equipped to tackle challenges and stay positive.

By maintaining a positive attitude and mindset, you can stay motivated and focused on your goals, even when things don't go as planned. With a little effort and determination, you can achieve success and reach your goals.

The second degree is developing a plan.

"Don't wait for opportunities to find you. Create them instead."

"The doors will be opened to those who are bold enough to knock." Success comes to those who act. Once you have set your goals, it is important to create a plan that will help you achieve them. This plan should include specific steps and deadlines for each goal, as well as a timeline for completing them. The first step in developing a plan is to identify the problem that needs to be addressed. This involves thoroughly understanding the situation, the stakeholders involved, and the potential consequences of not addressing the problem. It may be necessary to conduct research, gather data, and consult with experts to fully understand the problem.

Setting goals and objectives involves defining specific, measurable, achievable, relevant, and time-bound targets that you aim to achieve, and creating a plan for how you will work towards achieving them. Once the problem has been identified, the next step is to set specific goals and objectives for the plan. These goals and objectives should be specific, measurable, achievable, relevant, and time-bound. They should be aligned with the overall vision and mission of the organisation, and should be based on a thorough understanding of the problem and the resources available to address it.

Develop strategies and tactics effectively to pursue your goals and achieve your desired outcomes. Once the goals and objectives have been established, the next step is to develop the strategies and tactics that will be used to achieve them. This may involve brainstorming and collaboration with stakeholders, as well as conducting research and analysis to identify the most effective approaches. The strategies and tactics should be carefully designed to align with the goals and objectives, and should be feasible within the available resources.

An action plan is a detailed, step-by-step plan that outlines the tasks and resources needed to achieve a specific goal or objective, and identifies who is responsible for completing each step. With the strategies and tactics in place, the next step is to create an action plan that outlines the specific steps that will be taken to implement the plan. This plan should include a timeline, with specific milestones and deadlines for each action item. It should also identify the resources that will be needed, such as personnel, materials, and funding, and should specify who will be responsible for each action item.

Implementing and monitoring a plan involves carrying out the tasks and activities identified in the plan and regularly tracking progress to ensure that the plan is being followed and that the goal or objective is being achieved. This may involve making adjustments to the plan as needed to ensure its effectiveness and efficiency. Once the action plan is in place, the next step is to begin implementing the plan. This will involve coordinating the efforts of all stakeholders and ensuring that each action item is completed on time and within budget. It will also be necessary to monitor the progress of the plan, and to make any necessary adjustments based on the results. This may involve conducting regular meetings, collecting and analysing data, and providing feedback to stakeholders.

Evaluating and adjusting a plan involves regularly reviewing the progress made towards achieving the goal or objective and making changes to the plan as needed to ensure that it remains effective and relevant.

After the plan has been implemented, it is important to evaluate its effectiveness and to make any necessary adjustments. This may involve conducting a formal evaluation, using metrics and benchmarks to assess the plan's performance against the goals and objectives. Based on the results of the evaluation, it may be necessary to make changes to the plan, such as revising the strategies and tactics, or adjusting the timeline and resources. The goal of this final step is to ensure that the plan continues to be effective and continues to address the problem in the most effective way possible.

Communicating a plan involves sharing the details of the plan with the relevant stakeholders, such as team members, management, or clients, and ensuring that everyone understands their role and responsibilities in achieving the goal or objective. Effective communication of the plan can help to ensure that everyone is aligned and working towards the same goal, and can help to avoid misunderstandings or miscommunications. Effective communication is essential to the success of any plan. Throughout the planning process, it is important to keep stakeholders informed and engaged, and to provide regular updates on the progress of the plan. This may involve holding meetings, sending out newsletters, and using other forms of communication to keep stakeholders informed and involved. In addition to communicating with stakeholders, it is also important to communicate the plan to the broader community. This may involve creating marketing materials, such as brochures, flyers, and website content, to raise awareness about the plan and its objectives. It may also involve working with the media to share information about the plan and to generate support for its implementation.

Securing resources and support involves identifying and acquiring the necessary resources and support needed to implement and successfully achieve a plan or goal. This may include financial resources, materials, equipment, personnel, or other types of support, and may involve negotiations or other efforts to secure these resources. Implementing a plan often requires significant resources, such as personnel, materials, and funding.

It is important to secure these resources in advance, and to develop a plan for how they will be used. This may involve working with other organisations, seeking out grants and funding opportunities, and identifying other sources of support. In addition to securing resources, it is also important to secure the support of key stakeholders. This may involve building partnerships and alliances, engaging with community leaders, and involving stakeholders in the planning process. By involving stakeholders and gaining their support, it is possible to build a stronger foundation for the plan and to increase its chances of success. Reviewing and updating a plan involves periodically reviewing the progress made towards achieving the goal or objective and making any necessary changes to the plan to ensure that it remains effective and relevant.

No plan is static, and it is important to review and update the regular basis. This may involve conducting regular meetings, reviewing data and performance metrics, and soliciting feedback from stakeholders.

By regularly reviewing and updating the plan, it is possible to ensure that it remains relevant, effective, and aligned with the organisation's overall vision and mission. Additionally, it is important to be prepared for potential challenges and obstacles that may arise during the implementation of the plan.

By regularly reviewing and updating the plan, it is possible to identify potential risks and to develop contingency plans to address them. This can help to prevent unexpected setbacks and to ensure that the plan remains on track.

Celebrating successes and recognizing achievements involves acknowledging and celebrating the progress and accomplishments made towards achieving a goal or objective, and recognizing the contributions of individuals or teams who played a role in achieving these successes. This can help to boost morale and motivation, and can create a positive, supportive environment that encourages continued success. It is important to celebrate successes and recognize the achievements of those involved in implementing the plan. This may involve holding special events, recognizing individuals and teams for their contributions, and sharing stories of success with the broader community. By acknowledging the hard work and dedication of those involved in the plan, it is possible to build morale, foster a sense of accomplishment, and motivate everyone to continue working towards the goals and objectives of the plan.

Maintaining momentum and sustaining the plan involves keeping the focus on achieving the goal or objective and taking actions to ensure that the plan is implemented and progress is made towards achieving the desired outcome. This may involve continuing to communicate and coordinate with team members and stakeholders, tracking progress, and making any necessary adjustments to the plan as needed. Sustaining the plan also involves staying motivated and committed to achieving the goal, and staying focused on the benefits and value of the plan to the organisation or individual. Once the plan has been implemented, it is important to maintain momentum and to sustain the efforts that have been put in place. This may involve conducting regular check-ins and progress updates, providing ongoing support and resources to those involved in the plan, and staying engaged with stakeholders.

It is also important to continue to monitor the effectiveness of the plan and to make any necessary adjustments. This may involve gathering and analysing data, soliciting feedback from stakeholders, and conducting regular evaluations to assess the plan's performance against its goals and objectives. By regularly reviewing and updating the plan, it is possible to ensure that it remains relevant, effective, and aligned with the organisation's overall vision and mission.Finally, it is important to build on the successes of the plan and to continue to grow and evolve. This may involve identifying new opportunities, developing new strategies and tactics, and engaging with new stakeholders. By remaining open to change and adaptability, it is possible to continue to build on the successes of the plan and to ensure its long-term sustainability.

The third degree is taking action.

"The greatest risk in life is not taking action towards your dreams."

"Action is the foundational key to all success". Simply creating a plan is not enough – you must take action and put your plan into motion. This means making a commitment to yourself and following through on your plan, even when it gets tough or you face challenges.

Assembling the team and assigning roles involves identifying the people who will be responsible for implementing the plan and assigning specific tasks and responsibilities to each member of the team.

This may involve evaluating the skills and expertise of team members and assigning tasks that align with their strengths and capabilities, and may also involve delegating leadership roles and establishing clear lines of communication and accountability within the team.

The first step in taking action on a plan is to assemble a team of individuals who will be responsible for implementing the plan. This team should be composed of individuals with the necessary skills, knowledge, and expertise to successfully execute the plan.

It is important to clearly define the roles and responsibilities of each team member, and to ensure that everyone understands their role and how it contributes to the success of the plan.

Once the team has been assembled, the next step is to create a timeline and schedule for implementing the plan. This timeline should include specific milestones and deadlines for each action item, and should take into account the availability and capacity of the team members.

Creating a timeline and schedule involves establishing a plan for when specific tasks and activities will be completed in order to achieve the goal or objective, and organising these tasks and activities into a logical sequence.

It is important to establish clear expectations for when each action item should be completed, and to regularly review and update the timeline as needed. A timeline and schedule can help to ensure that the plan is implemented in a timely and efficient manner, and can help to keep the team on track and focused on achieving the desired outcome.

Effective communication is essential to the success of any plan. Developing a communication plan helps to ensure that all stakeholders are informed and aligned, and can help to avoid misunderstandings or miscommunications.

It is important to develop a communication plan that outlines how the team will communicate with each other, with stakeholders, and with the broader community.

A communication plan is a detailed plan that outlines how information will be shared and communicated within an organisation or team, including the methods and channels that will be used, the frequency of communication, and the specific messages that will be conveyed.

This plan should include details on the frequency and format of communication, as well as the specific channels and tools that will be used.

It is also important to establish clear protocols for responding to questions and concerns, and to ensure that everyone is kept informed and engaged throughout the implementation process.

Implementing a plan often requires significant resources, such as personnel, materials, and funding. Securing necessary resources involves identifying and acquiring the materials, equipment, financial resources, or other types of support needed to implement and successfully achieve a plan or goal. It is important to secure these resources in advance, and to develop a plan for how they will be used.

This may involve working with other organisations, seeking out grants and funding opportunities, and identifying other sources of support. This may also involve negotiations or other efforts to secure these resources, and may also involve budgeting and financial planning to ensure that the necessary resources are available.

In addition to securing resources, it is also important to ensure that the team has the necessary tools, equipment, and technology to successfully execute the plan. This may involve purchasing or renting equipment, training team members on the use of new tools, and ensuring that everyone has access to the resources they need to complete their tasks.

Once the plan has been implemented, it is important to monitor progress and to make any necessary adjustments. To monitor progress and adjust as needed, it is helpful to regularly assess how well a plan or project is progressing and make any necessary changes to stay on track and achieve desired outcomes.

This may involve conducting regular meetings, collecting and analysing data, and providing feedback to team members. By regularly reviewing and updating the plan, it is possible to identify potential challenges and to develop contingency plans to address them. This can help to prevent unexpected setbacks and to ensure that the plan remains on track.

It is important to celebrate successes and recognize the achievements of those involved in implementing the plan. Celebrating successes and recognizing achievements helps to motivate and engage team members, boost morale, and foster a positive and supportive work culture.

This may involve holding special events, recognizing individuals and teams for their contributions, and sharing stories of success with the broader community. By acknowledging the hard work and dedication of those involved in the plan, it is possible to build morale, foster a sense of accomplishment, and motivate everyone to continue working towards the goals and objectives of the plan.

After the plan has been implemented, it is important to evaluate its effectiveness and to make any necessary adjustments.To evaluate and adjust a plan, it is important to regularly assess its effectiveness and make any necessary changes to ensure that it is still relevant and aligned with the goals and objectives it is intended to achieve. This may involve conducting a formal evaluation, using metrics and benchmarks to assess the plan's performance against the goals and objectives. Based on the results of the evaluation, it may be necessary to make changes to the plan, such as revising the strategies and tactics, or adjusting the timeline and resources. The goal of this step is to ensure that the plan continues to be effective and continues to address the problem in the most effective way possible.

Once the plan has been implemented and evaluated, it is important to communicate the results and learnings to stakeholders and the broader community.

Communicating the results and learnings from a project or plan helps to share valuable information and insights with stakeholders, and can inform future decision making and planning efforts. This may involve creating reports and presentations, sharing success stories, and providing updates on the impact of the plan. It is also important to engage with stakeholders and to solicit their feedback on the plan, to ensure that it continues to align with their needs and priorities. It is important to sustain and build on the efforts that have been put in place through the plan.To sustain and build on a plan, it is important to continually review and assess its effectiveness and make any necessary adjustments to ensure that it is still relevant and aligned with the goals and objectives it is intended to achieve, and to identify opportunities for improvement and growth. This may involve continuing to monitor and evaluate the plan, and making any necessary adjustments. It may also involve identifying new opportunities and developing new strategies to continue to address the problem and achieve the goals and objectives of the plan. By maintaining a focus on sustainability and continuous improvement, it is possible to ensure that the plan remains relevant and effective over time. "The road to success is paved with small, consistent actions."

The fourth degree is persistence.

"Persistence is the fuel that keeps the fire of success burning bright."

"It's not about how many times you fall down, it's about how many times you get back up with persistence and determination." Success rarely comes easily, and it is important to keep pushing forward even when you face setbacks or obstacles. This means staying focused and determined, and not giving up on your goals. The first step in being persistent is to identify the obstacles and challenges that are standing in the way of achieving your goals. To identify the obstacles and challenges that may impact the progress or success of a plan or project, it is helpful to regularly assess the current environment and consider any potential risks or challenges that may arise. This may involve conducting a thorough assessment of your current situation, your resources, and the external factors that may be impacting your ability to progress. By understanding the obstacles and challenges that you are facing, it is possible to develop strategies to overcome them and to move forward. Once you have identified the obstacles and challenges that are standing in your way, the next step is to develop a plan and set specific goals to overcome them. To develop a plan and set goals, it is important to clearly define the desired outcomes and identify the steps and resources needed to achieve them, as well as to establish measurable benchmarks to track progress and assess the effectiveness of the plan.

This may involve setting short-term and long-term goals, breaking larger goals down into smaller, more manageable steps, and identifying the resources and support that you will need to achieve your goals. By setting clear goals and developing a plan, you can create a roadmap for success and stay focused and motivated on your path.

Persistence requires focus and motivation. It is important to stay focused on your goals, to remain committed to your plan, and to continue to push forward even when faced with obstacles and challenges. To stay focused and motivated, it can be helpful to set clear and specific goals, break large tasks into smaller, more manageable chunks, and establish a regular routine or schedule to help prioritise and organise work.

Additionally, taking breaks and engaging in activities that promote relaxation and well-being can help to sustain focus and motivation over time. This may require regular self-reflection, setting aside time for self-care and personal growth, and seeking out support and guidance from others. By staying focused and motivated, you can overcome obstacles and challenges, and continue to move forward towards your goals.

Being persistent does not mean sticking to the same plan and strategy regardless of the circumstances. It is important to be adaptable and open to change, and to be willing to adjust your plan and approach as needed.

Being adaptable and open to change involves being willing and able to adjust plans or approaches as needed in response to new information, shifting priorities, or unexpected challenges, in order to achieve desired outcomes and remain agile and responsive in an ever-changing environment.

This may involve conducting regular reviews and evaluations, soliciting feedback from others, and being open to new ideas and perspectives. By being adaptable and open to change, you can remain flexible and responsive to the changing landscape, and continue to make progress towards your goals.

Persistence often requires a positive mindset and a focus on the end result. It is important to stay positive, even in the face of setbacks and challenges, and to remain focused on the ultimate goal that you are working towards. To stay positive and focused on the end result, it can be helpful to regularly remind oneself of the purpose and value of the work being done, and to set small, achievable goals along the way to help maintain motivation and momentum.

Additionally, seeking support and encouragement from others, and finding ways to stay engaged and inspired, can also help to maintain a positive outlook and stay focused on the ultimate objective. This may involve regularly reminding yourself of the reasons why you are pursuing your goals, and staying motivated and inspired by the potential rewards and benefits of achieving them.

By staying positive and focused on the end result, you can maintain the drive and determination needed to persist in the face of obstacles.

Ultimately, being persistent means never giving up. It means continuing to push forward, even when faced with obstacles and challenges, and remaining committed to your goals and your plan. This may require perseverance, resilience, and determination, but the rewards of persistence can be significant.

To persevere and never give up, it is important to stay focused on the end goal, even when faced with setbacks or challenges, and to maintain a positive attitude and commitment to finding solutions and working towards success.

This can involve seeking support and resources, being open to new ideas and approaches, and continually adjusting and adapting as needed to overcome obstacles and achieve desired outcomes. By persevering and never giving up, you can achieve your goals, overcome obstacles, and achieve success. "The road to success is never easy, but with persistence and hard work, you can reach your destination"

The fifth degree is discipline.

"As an entrepreneur, discipline is the key to staying focused, motivated, and productive."

"Discipline is the cornerstone of any successful business. Without it, you'll struggle to reach your goals and achieve lasting success." In order to achieve success, you must be disciplined in your approach. This means being consistent and sticking to your plan, even when it is difficult or you don't feel like it.

Discipline helps to promote good behaviour and habits by establishing clear expectations and consequences for actions, and by providing structure and consistent guidance to help individuals develop self-control and make responsible choices.

This can involve setting rules and boundaries, establishing routines and schedules, and providing positive reinforcement and consequences as needed to encourage desired behaviours and discourage undesirable ones. By setting clear rules and expectations, and consistently enforcing them, individuals can learn to make positive choices and avoid negative behaviours.

Discipline helps to build self-control and self-regulation by providing structure and consistent guidance that

28

helps individuals develop the ability to make responsible decisions and manage their own behaviour. This can involve setting clear rules and expectations, establishing routines and schedules, and providing positive reinforcement and consequences as needed to encourage desired behaviours and discourage undesirable ones.

As individuals learn to regulate their own behaviour and make responsible choices, they can develop greater self-control and self-regulation skills. When individuals are able to control their own actions and emotions, they are better able to make responsible decisions and achieve their goals.

Discipline fosters a sense of responsibility and accountability by establishing clear expectations and consequences for actions, and by providing consistent guidance and feedback that helps individuals understand the impact of their behaviour on themselves and others. This can involve setting rules and boundaries, establishing routines and schedules, and providing positive reinforcement and consequences as needed to encourage desired behaviours and discourage undesirable ones.

 As individuals learn to take responsibility for their actions and understand the consequences of their behaviour, they can develop a stronger sense of accountability. By holding individuals accountable for their actions, discipline encourages them to take ownership of their behaviour and the consequences of their actions.

Discipline promotes respect for authority and the rules of society by helping individuals learn to follow established rules and guidelines, and by providing structure and guidance that
helps them understand the importance of respecting authority and the rules that govern behaviour within a community or society.

This can involve setting clear expectations and consequences for actions, establishing routines and schedules, and providing consistent feedback and guidance to help individuals develop an understanding of and appreciation for the role that rules and authority play in maintaining order and harmony within a community. When individuals understand and follow the rules, they show respect for those who have authority over them and for the social norms that help to maintain order and stability.

Discipline helps to create a safe and orderly environment by establishing clear expectations and consequences for behaviour, and by providing structure and guidance that helps individuals learn to manage their own behaviour and make responsible choices. This can involve setting rules and boundaries, establishing routines and schedules, and providing positive reinforcement and consequences as needed to encourage desired behaviours and discourage undesirable ones.

By promoting self-control and respect for authority, discipline can help to create a safe and orderly environment that is conducive to learning and personal growth By setting and enforcing rules, individuals can help to prevent conflicts and disruptions, and create a space where everyone can feel safe and secure.

Discipline can improve performance and productivity by providing structure and guidance that helps individuals focus their efforts, set clear goals, and manage their time and resources effectively. This can involve establishing routines and schedules, setting clear expectations and consequences for actions, and providing feedback and support to help individuals develop skills and habits that enable them to work efficiently and effectively.

By helping individuals stay organised, focused, and motivated, discipline can help to improve performance and productivity. By setting goals and holding individuals accountable for their actions, discipline can help individuals to stay focused and motivated, and to achieve success in their personal and professional lives.

Discipline fosters a sense of belonging and community by establishing clear rules and expectations for behaviour, which helps to create a cohesive and harmonious environment where individuals feel supported and connected to one another.

By following the rules and expectations set forth within a community, individuals demonstrate their commitment to the group and its values, which can strengthen the bonds of social cohesion and encourage a sense of unity and belonging. In this way, discipline can be a powerful tool for fostering a sense of belonging and community within any social group.

When individuals follow the rules and contribute to the greater good, they can build strong relationships and a sense of belonging within their social groups. By working together and supporting each other, individuals can create a positive and inclusive community.

Discipline helps to develop a growth mindset by encouraging individuals to set goals, work towards them, and persevere in the face of challenges and setbacks.
By consistently practising self-control, perseverance, and the ability to delay gratification, individuals can cultivate the mental habits and attitudes that are necessary for a growth mindset. With a growth mindset,

individuals believe that their abilities and potential can be developed through effort and learning, rather than being fixed at birth.

As a result, discipline can be a powerful tool for helping individuals to develop a growth mindset and to achieve their full potential. When individuals face challenges and obstacles, discipline can help them to persevere and overcome those obstacles. By setting goals, working hard, and making progress, individuals can develop a mindset that is focused on growth and improvement, rather than on limitations and setbacks.

Discipline can help improve mental and emotional well-being by providing a sense of structure and stability, helping to develop self-control and self-regulation, and allowing individuals to achieve their goals and feel a sense of accomplishment. By setting boundaries and maintaining a sense of order and control, individuals can reduce stress and anxiety, and improve their overall mental and emotional health.

Discipline can foster independence and self-reliance by teaching individuals to take responsibility for their actions and make decisions for themselves, encouraging them to think for themselves and solve problems on their own, and helping them develop self-motivation and self-discipline. By setting goals and working towards them, individuals can develop the skills and confidence they need to take control of their own lives and make their own decisions.

Discipline can promote a sense of accomplishment and satisfaction by helping individuals set and work towards goals, allowing them to see progress and improvement, and providing a sense of pride and accomplishment when they achieve their goals. When individuals set goals, work hard, and achieve their objectives, they can experience a sense of pride and accomplishment that can boost their self-esteem and overall happiness.

Discipline can help to build character and integrity by teaching individuals to adhere to their values and principles, encouraging honesty and integrity in their actions and decisions, and helping them to develop self-control and self-regulation. By consistently choosing to do the right thing, even when it is difficult, individuals can develop strong moral character and a sense of integrity that can guide their actions and decisions.

Discipline can lead to greater success and fulfilment in life by helping individuals set and work towards goals, develop healthy habits and routines, and make responsible and effective decisions, which can all contribute to a more fulfilling and successful life. By setting goals, working hard, and staying focused and motivated, individuals can achieve their dreams and find fulfilment in their personal and professional lives. By practising discipline, individuals can create the life they want and reach their full potential.

Discipline refers to the practice of training oneself to follow rules, adhere to a set of values or principles, and engage in behaviours that lead to improvement and self-control.
Discipline refers to the practice of training individuals to follow rules and standards, and to behave in accordance with certain expectations. It involves setting rules and expectations, and consistently enforcing them in order to promote good behaviour and prevent negative actions.

The benefits of discipline include improved self-control and self-regulation, a sense of accomplishment and satisfaction, greater success and fulfilment in life, and the development of character and integrity. Discipline offers many benefits, both to individuals and to society as a whole.

For individuals, discipline can improve mental and emotional well-being, foster independence and self-reliance, and lead to greater success and fulfilment in life. For society, discipline helps to promote respect for authority and the rules of society, and can create a more cohesive and functional community.

The role of parents and caregivers in discipline: Parents and caregivers play a crucial role in teaching and enforcing discipline. By setting clear rules and expectations, and consistently enforcing them, parents and caregivers can help children to learn self-control and self-regulation, and to make positive choices.

The role of educators in discipline: Educators also play a critical role in teaching and enforcing discipline. By setting clear rules and expectations, and consistently enforcing them, educators can help students to learn self-control and self-regulation, and to make positive choices.

The role of the legal system in discipline: The legal system is also involved in enforcing discipline. By setting laws and rules, and holding individuals accountable for their actions, the legal system helps to promote good behaviour and prevent negative actions.

The challenges of discipline: Discipline can sometimes be challenging, both for individuals and for society. It can be difficult to set and enforce rules consistently, and individuals may sometimes resist or challenge discipline. It is important to approach discipline in a fair and balanced way, and to consider the needs and perspectives of all involved.

The relationship between discipline and punishment: Discipline and punishment are often closely related, but they are not the same thing. Discipline involves training individuals to follow rules and standards, and to make positive choices.

Punishment, on the other hand, involves imposing a consequence for negative actions or behaviours. While punishment can be a part of discipline, it is not the only aspect of it, and it should not be used as the sole means of enforcing discipline.

The role of rewards and positive reinforcement in discipline: In addition to punishment, discipline can also involve the use of rewards and positive reinforcement. By praising and rewarding good behaviour, individuals can be encouraged to make positive choices and avoid negative actions.
The role of communication in discipline: Effective communication is key to successful discipline. By clearly communicating rules and expectations, and listening to and addressing the concerns and perspectives of those involved, individuals can foster a sense of understanding and cooperation, and can more effectively enforce discipline.

The role of consistency in discipline: Consistency is also important in effective discipline. By setting and enforcing rules consistently, individuals can help to create a sense of predictability and stability, and can more effectively teach and reinforce good behaviour.

The role of boundaries in discipline: Setting boundaries is also crucial in discipline. By defining clear limits and expectations, individuals can help to create a sense of order and control, and can more effectively enforce discipline.

The role of empathy and understanding in discipline: Finally, empathy and understanding are also important in effective discipline. By considering the needs and perspectives of those involved, and by showing empathy and understanding, individuals can create a more positive and supportive environment for discipline.

Discipline is an important aspect of both work and life. In the workplace, discipline can help to promote good behaviour and habits, improve performance and productivity, and foster a safe and orderly environment. It can also help to build self-control and self-regulation, and to develop a growth mindset.

In personal life, discipline can help individuals to make positive choices, build self-control and self-regulation, and achieve their goals. It can also improve mental and emotional well-being, foster independence and self-reliance, and lead to greater success and fulfilment.

Overall, discipline is a crucial tool for achieving success and fulfilment in both work and life. By setting rules and expectations, and consistently enforcing them, individuals can learn to make positive choices and avoid negative actions, and can create a more positive and fulfilling life for themselves and those around them.

Discipline and goal-setting: Discipline is closely linked to goal-setting. By setting goals and working towards them, individuals can develop the discipline and focus they need to achieve success.

Discipline and motivation: Discipline is also essential for maintaining motivation. By setting goals, creating a plan, and staying focused and committed, individuals can stay motivated and on track towards achieving their goals.

Discipline and perseverance: Discipline is also key to persevering in the face of obstacles and challenges. By staying focused and committed, individuals can maintain their discipline and continue working towards their goals, even when faced with setbacks and challenges.

Discipline and hard work: Discipline also involves hard work and dedication. By putting in the effort and working hard, individuals can develop the discipline they need to achieve their goals.

Discipline and time management: Discipline is also important for effective time management. By setting priorities, creating a schedule, and staying focused and organised, individuals can use their time more effectively and make progress towards their goals. Discipline and focus: Discipline is also closely linked to focus. By staying focused on their goals and avoiding distractions, individuals can maintain their discipline and make steady progress towards achieving success.

Discipline and success: Ultimately, discipline is an essential component of success. By setting goals, working hard, staying focused, and persevering, individuals can develop the discipline they need to achieve their goals and find success in their personal and professional lives.
Discipline and self-improvement: Discipline is also important for self-improvement. By setting goals, working hard, and consistently striving to improve, individuals can develop the discipline they need to grow and evolve as individuals.
Discipline and personal growth: Discipline is also essential for personal growth and development. By setting goals, working hard, and staying focused and committed, individuals can develop the discipline they need to grow and evolve as individuals.

Discipline and success in relationships: Discipline is also important for success in relationships. By setting boundaries, communicating openly and honestly, and staying committed to the relationship, individuals can develop the discipline they need to build and maintain strong, healthy relationships.

Discipline and success in the workplace: Discipline is also critical for success in the workplace. By setting goals, working hard, and staying focused and committed, individuals can develop the discipline they need to excel in their careers and achieve their professional goals. Discipline and success in school: Discipline is also essential for success in school. By setting goals, working hard, and staying focused and committed, students can develop the discipline they need to excel in their studies and achieve their academic goals.

Discipline and success in sports: Discipline is also crucial for success in sports. By setting goals, working hard, and staying focused and committed, athletes can develop the discipline they need to excel in their sport and achieve their athletic goals. "The most successful entrepreneurs are those who have the discipline to stay focused and work towards their goals every day."

The sixth degree is hard work.

"The only way to achieve greatness is through hard work and dedication."

When I was a child growing up in N.Macedonia my grandfather was a hard worker who worked over thirty years in construction in Switzerland, always saying "hard work never killed anyone." "Hard work is the only way to turn your dreams into reality." Success requires effort, and the more effort you put in, the greater your chances of success will be. This means putting in long hours and putting your all into your work, even when it is difficult or you don't feel like it.

In today's fast-paced world, it's easy to get caught up in the rat race and forget the value of hard work. But the truth is, hard work is an essential ingredient for success in any field. Whether you're an athlete, a business person, or an artist, the ability to put in long hours and stay focused on your goals is essential for achieving your dreams. Hard work is important in business and life because it allows individuals to achieve their goals, improve their skills and knowledge, and create opportunities for success.

Hard work may not always be easy, but it is always rewarding. By putting in the effort to overcome obstacles and reach your goals, you can gain a sense of accomplishment and pride in your achievements. Additionally, hard work can lead to tangible rewards such as promotions, raises, and accolades. The rewards of hard work for entrepreneurs include increased productivity, personal satisfaction, career advancement, and financial success.

In addition to the rewards of hard work, there are also many benefits that come with putting in the effort. For one, hard work can lead to personal growth and development. By challenging yourself and pushing beyond your comfort zone, you can learn new skills and gain new perspectives on life. As an entrepreneur, the benefits of hard work include the ability to achieve one's business goals, create value for customers, and potentially earn financial rewards.

One of the key qualities of successful people is their ability to persevere, even in the face of adversity. When things don't go as planned, it can be tempting to give up and move on to something else. But those who are able to persevere and keep working hard are often the ones who end up achieving their goals. As an entrepreneur, the power of perseverance allows individuals to overcome challenges and setbacks, stay focused on their goals, and eventually achieve success in their business endeavours.

Of course, no journey to success is without its obstacles. There will always be challenges and setbacks along the way. The key is to not let these obstacles discourage you or stop you from pursuing your dreams. Instead, use them as opportunities to learn and grow, and keep pushing forward with determination and hard work. In entrepreneurship, overcoming obstacles involves identifying and addressing challenges and setbacks in order to move forward and achieve success. This often requires persistence, adaptability, and the ability to learn from mistakes. While hard work is essential for achieving success, it's not enough on its own. To truly excel in your field, you need to be passionate about what you do. When you're passionate about something, you're more motivated to put in the extra effort and stay focused on your goals, even when things get tough. In everything we do either at work or at home, passion can play a vital role in driving us to pursue our goals with enthusiasm and determination, leading to greater success and fulfilment.A hard-working attitude can lead to increased productivity, personal satisfaction, and success in both one's career and personal life. It can also be a valuable trait that is respected and admired by others.In the end, the rewards of hard work go far beyond any tangible rewards or accolades. When you have a hard-working attitude and a commitment to excellence, you'll find that you're more fulfilled and satisfied in your personal and professional life. And that's a reward that money can't buy.

Another crucial component of hard work is self-discipline. Self-discipline is important because it helps individuals to control their actions and make positive choices, leading to greater self-control, self-esteem, and success in various endeavours. In order to be successful, you need to be able to control your impulses and focus on your goals.

This requires discipline in your daily habits, such as maintaining a regular work schedule, avoiding procrastination, and staying organised. By developing self-discipline, you can improve your productivity and increase your chances of success.

Another important quality for hard workers is determination. Determination is important because it allows individuals to stay focused on their goals and work towards achieving them, despite facing challenges or setbacks. It is a key factor in successful problem-solving and decision-making.

This means having the resilience and persistence to keep going, even when things are tough. When you're determined to succeed, you're willing to put in the extra effort and make the necessary sacrifices to reach your goals. This determination can be a powerful force that helps you overcome obstacles and achieve success.

Having a positive attitude is another key factor in hard work and success. When you approach your work with a positive outlook, you're more likely to stay motivated and focused on your goals. A positive attitude can also help you stay optimistic and resilient in the face of challenges.

A positive attitude can have numerous benefits, including improved mental and physical health, increased motivation and productivity, better relationships with others, and increased resilience in the face of challenges. By maintaining a positive outlook, you can increase your chances of success and enjoy a happier and more fulfilling life.

While hard work is often a solitary pursuit, it's also important to recognize the role of collaboration in achieving success. The power of collaboration lies in the ability of individuals to work together towards a common goal, leveraging their diverse skills and knowledge to achieve greater results than they could individually. Collaboration can lead to increased innovation, productivity, and success. By working together with others, you can combine your strengths and expertise to accomplish more than you could on your own. Collaboration can also provide valuable opportunities for learning and growth, as you share ideas and learn from each other.

Having a mentor or role model can also be a valuable asset in your journey to success. A good mentor can be a valuable resource and source of inspiration for anyone seeking to grow and succeed in their career or personal endeavours.

Mentors play an important role and can provide guidance, advice, and support, helping you navigate the challenges of hard work and achieve your goals. By seeking out mentors and learning from their experiences, you can gain valuable insights and avoid common pitfalls on your path to success.

One final aspect of hard work that's worth mentioning is the value of lifelong learning. In today's fast-changing world, it's important to stay on top of new developments and trends in your field. By continuing to learn and grow, you can stay competitive and continue to achieve success throughout your career. Whether it's through formal education or on-the-job training, lifelong learning is an essential part of the hard-working mindset.

An important aspect of hard work is the ability to set goals and work towards achieving them. By setting clear, specific, and achievable goals, you can provide yourself with direction and motivation. When you have a goal to work towards, you're more likely to stay focused and put in the effort necessary to succeed.

In order to be successful, you need to be able to manage your time effectively. This means setting priorities, making plans, and staying organised. By managing your time wisely, you can maximise your productivity and avoid becoming overwhelmed. With good time management, you'll be able to accomplish more in less time, which will help you achieve your goals and succeed in your field.

Another key factor in hard work and success is the concept of a growth mindset. This means having a belief that you can improve and grow, rather than being limited by fixed abilities. When you have a growth mindset, you're more likely to take on challenges, learn from your mistakes, and persevere in the face of adversity. By adopting a growth mindset, you can open yourself up to new possibilities and opportunities for success.

In addition to determination and perseverance, another essential quality for hard workers is resilience. This means being able to bounce back from setbacks and failures, and continue to work towards your goals. With resilience, you can overcome obstacles and continue to move forward, even when things don't go as planned. By developing resilience, you can increase your chances of success and achieve your goals.

It's important to recognize the role of support in hard work and success. No one achieves their goals entirely on their own, and having a support system can make all the difference. This might include friends and family members who provide emotional support, or colleagues and mentors who offer advice and guidance. By seeking out and accepting support, you can increase your chances of success and make your journey to success a little bit easier.

Another key component of hard work and success is adaptability. In today's rapidly changing world, it's essential to be able to adapt to new situations and challenges. By being open to change and willing to learn, you can stay flexible and responsive to the changing needs of your field. With adaptability, you can continue to succeed and grow, even as the world around you changes.

Having a positive work ethic is another important aspect of hard work and success. This means having a commitment to excellence, and a willingness to put in the effort necessary to achieve your goals. With a positive work ethic, you're more likely to stay motivated and focused on your work, and to maintain high standards of quality and performance. By developing a positive work ethic, you can increase your chances of success and enjoy a more fulfilling career.

In order to succeed, you need to be able to motivate yourself to work hard. This means being able to set goals and work towards them, even when there are no external rewards or incentives. With self-motivation, you can stay focused and committed to your goals, and keep pushing yourself to achieve your full potential. By developing self-motivation, you can increase your chances of success and enjoy a more fulfilling and rewarding career.

Finally, having an optimistic attitude can also be a valuable asset in hard work and success. When you're optimistic, you're more likely to see the potential in challenges and setbacks, and to find ways to overcome them. With optimism, you can maintain a positive outlook, even in the face of adversity. By developing an optimistic attitude, you can increase your chances of success and enjoy a happier and more fulfilling life. The difference between those who succeed and those who don't is often simply the willingness to put in the hard work required. Hard work is the foundation of any successful venture. Without it, you'll struggle to achieve your goals and reach your full potential. "The most successful people are those who are willing to put in the hard work and dedication required to reach their goals."

The seventh degree is learning from failure.

"Failures are not the end, they are the beginning of a new journey."

"It's not how many times you fall, it's how you get up that determines the outcome." I had several failures in life. I had failures in two marriages and one business startup in which I lost almost everything and also took me years to recover."Failures are not a reason to give up, they are a reason to try harder and be better." Failures are not a reflection of your worth, they are a sign that you are trying new things and taking risks. Every failure is an opportunity to learn and grow. No one achieves success without facing setbacks or failures along the way. It is important to learn from these failures and use them as opportunities to grow and improve.

Failure is a natural part of life, and it is especially common in the world of business. In this book, we will explore the topic of learning from failure, both in business and in life. We will look at how failure can be a valuable opportunity for growth and learning, and how we can use it to our advantage. One of the first steps in learning from failure is to embrace it as a learning opportunity. Embracing failure as a learning opportunity involves viewing failures as opportunities to learn and grow, rather than as personal failures or setbacks.

This mindset can help individuals to learn from their mistakes and make better decisions in the future, leading to greater success and fulfilment. This can be difficult, especially if we are used to thinking of failure as something to be avoided at all costs. However, when we embrace failure as a learning opportunity, we open ourselves up to a world of possibilities. We can learn from our mistakes, and use that knowledge to improve and grow. Another important step in learning from failure is to take responsibility for our mistakes. This means acknowledging that we are responsible for our own actions, and that we are the ones who must take the necessary steps to improve and grow. By taking responsibility for our failures, we show that we are willing to take ownership of our actions and learn from them. Reflection is an important part of learning from failure. It allows us to step back and think about what went wrong, and why. This can be a difficult process, especially if we are used to moving on quickly from our mistakes. However, by taking the time to reflect on our failures, we can gain valuable insights that can help us avoid making the same mistakes in the future. Another important step in learning from failure is to seek feedback from others. This can be especially valuable because it gives us a different perspective on our failures. By seeking feedback from others, we can learn from their experiences and gain new insights into our own failures.

Having a growth mindset is crucial for learning from failure. A growth mindset is the belief that we can improve and grow, regardless of our current abilities or circumstances. By developing a growth mindset, we can overcome the fear of failure and embrace it as a learning opportunity.

In addition to learning from our own failures, we can also learn from the failures of others. By studying the successes and failures of others, we can gain valuable insights and lessons that we can apply to our own lives and businesses.

After we have reflected on our failures and sought feedback from others, the next step is to create a plan for improvement. This plan should outline specific steps that we can take to avoid making the same mistakes in the future. By creating a plan for improvement, we can turn our failures into opportunities for growth and learning.

Once we have created a plan for improvement, the next step is to take action on it. This means implementing the specific steps outlined in our plan, and taking the necessary steps to avoid making the same mistakes in the future. By taking action on our plan, we can turn our failures into opportunities for growth and learning.

As we work to improve and grow, it is important to celebrate our progress. This can help to motivate us and keep us on track. By celebrating our progress, we can also gain a sense of accomplishment and satisfaction, which can help us to stay focused and motivated.

In conclusion, learning from failure is an important part of life and business. By embracing failure as a learning opportunity, taking responsibility for our mistakes, reflecting on our failures, seeking feedback from others, developing a growth mindset, learning from the failures of others, creating a plan for improvement, taking action on our plan, and celebrating our progress, we can turn our failures into opportunities for growth and learning.

By learning from our failures, we can become more resilient and better equipped to handle the challenges and obstacles that come our way. "Failures are not setbacks, they are stepping stones to success." The greatest leaders are those who have faced failure and used it as an opportunity to learn and grow.

The eighth degree is seeking help.

"Asking for help is a sign of strength, not weakness. It takes courage to admit that we need assistance and the willingness to seek it out shows that we value our own well-being and growth."

"Seeking help is a brave and responsible choice. It takes courage to admit that we need support and the willingness to seek it out shows that we are taking control of our own lives." There were many times in my life when I needed help. I always had great support and encouragement from family, friends and mentors. Without these support systems in place we feel lost and unable to move forward. It is part of life and everyone at some point in life is going through. It's okay to not have all the answers or to feel overwhelmed. Seeking help is a way to find solutions and gain support in times of need. Asking for help is an opportunity to learn and grow. It allows us to seek guidance from those who have more experience or knowledge, and can lead to personal and professional development. No one is an expert in everything, and it is important to seek help and advice from others who have more experience or knowledge in your field. This can be through mentors, coaches, or even just friends and colleagues.

Asking for support can also help you achieve your goals and improve your quality of life.

Whether you are working on a personal project or trying to overcome a challenge, having the support of others can make a big difference. It can provide you with motivation, encouragement, and the resources you need to succeed.

There are many situations in which it may be necessary to seek help and ask for support. When you are facing a difficult challenge or problem that you don't know how to solve. Whether it's a personal or professional issue, getting support from others can help you find a solution and move forward. When you are feeling overwhelmed or burnt out. If you are struggling to manage your responsibilities or feeling burnt out, it can be helpful to ask for support to lighten your workload or find ways to cope with stress. When you are experiencing a significant life change or transition, such as a move, a new job, or the loss of a loved one. These types of changes can be difficult to navigate, and seeking help and support can make the process easier.

Overall, if you are struggling with a problem or feeling overwhelmed, it is important to consider seeking help and asking for support. Even if you are not sure where to turn or what type of help you need, reaching out for support is a positive step towards improving your well-being and quality of life. Ultimately, the key is to find the type of help and support that works best for you. Don't be afraid to reach out for support and explore different options until you find what works for you. To find help and support, you can reach out to mental health professionals, participate in support groups, rely on the support of family and friends, utilise community resources, or use online resources.

To overcome fear and hesitation in asking for help, it can be helpful to remind yourself that seeking help is a sign of strength and self-awareness, focus on the benefits of getting support, and remind yourself that you are not alone in your struggles.

To communicate effectively when asking for help and support, it can be helpful to clearly and concisely express your needs and concerns, be specific about the type of help you are seeking, and be open and honest about your feelings.

To build trust and rapport with those from whom you seek help, it can be helpful to be open and honest, be respectful and considerate, listen actively, and follow through on any commitments or agreements you make.

To be open and honest when seeking help and support, it can be helpful to share your thoughts, feelings, and experiences honestly and openly, without hiding or minimising any important information.

To show gratitude and appreciation for those who offer help and support, it can be helpful to thank them directly and sincerely, express your appreciation in specific terms, and consider finding ways to pay it forward or support them in return.

It is important to consider different perspectives and seek advice from multiple sources when trying to solve a problem or make a decision, as this can help you to gain a more well-rounded understanding of the situation and potential solutions. Using available resources and support systems, such as seeking help from friends, family, or professionals, can be an effective way to address and overcome challenges.

Seeking help and asking for support can be a difficult process, especially if you are not used to doing it or if you feel like you should be able to handle things on your own. However, it is important to recognize that seeking help and asking for support is a sign of strength, not weakness. It takes courage to admit that you need help and to take the steps necessary to get it. Asking for support can also be an important part of the process of making improvements and achieving your goals. .

To continue on the topic of seeking help and asking for support, it is important to understand the potential benefits of doing so. By seeking help and asking for support, individuals can gain valuable insights, advice, and assistance from others who may have more experience or expertise in a particular area. This can help individuals overcome challenges and obstacles, improve their skills and knowledge, and achieve their goals more effectively.

In addition to these direct benefits, seeking help and asking for support can also foster a sense of connection and community. It can provide individuals with a sense of belonging and support from others who can understand and empathise with their situation. This can provide a much-needed source of emotional support and can help individuals feel less alone in their struggles. Furthermore, seeking help and asking for support can also serve as a model for others. By showing vulnerability and asking for help, individuals can inspire and encourage others to do the same. This can help create a culture of support and collaboration within a group or organisation, leading to better outcomes for everyone involved. In short, seeking help and asking for support can be a crucial step towards personal and professional success. It can provide individuals with the tools and support they need to overcome challenges, improve their skills, and achieve their goals. By taking the initiative to seek help and ask for support, individuals can set themselves on the path to success.

One potential challenge in seeking help and asking for support is finding the right person or people to turn to. It is important to consider who may be best suited to offer the kind of help or support that is needed. This may require some research and consideration of different options. For example, if an individual is struggling with a specific work-related challenge, they may want to seek out a mentor or colleague who has experience in that area. If they are dealing with a personal issue, they may want to seek out a friend, family member, or counsellor who can offer a listening ear and support. It can also be helpful to consider the potential drawbacks of seeking help from a particular person or group. For example, an individual may be hesitant to seek help from a colleague because they are worried about being judged or appearing weak. In this case, it may be helpful to weigh the potential risks and benefits and determine if seeking help from that particular person or group is the best course of action. Overall, it is important to take the time to carefully consider the options and find the right person or people to turn to for help and support. By doing so, individuals can increase the chances of receiving the help and support they need to overcome challenges and achieve their goals. Once an individual has identified the right person or people to turn to for help and support, it is important to communicate effectively when asking for help. This may require being specific and clear about what kind of help is needed, as well as being open and honest about the challenges and obstacles that are being faced.

It can also be helpful to communicate why the help and support is needed and what the individual hopes to achieve by seeking help. This can provide the person or people being asked for help with a better understanding of the situation and can help them offer more tailored and effective assistance.

In addition, it is important to be receptive to feedback and advice when asking for help. While individuals may have their own ideas about what they need, it is important to consider the perspectives and suggestions of others who may have more experience or expertise in the area. By being open to different viewpoints, individuals can expand their thinking and potentially find new and creative solutions to their challenges.

Overall, effective communication is key when seeking help and asking for support. By being clear and open in their communication, individuals can increase the chances of receiving the help and support they need to overcome challenges and achieve their goals.

The ninth degree is staying focused.

"The ability to stay focused is a key factor in the success of any entrepreneur. It allows us to stay on track and make progress towards our goals."

"As entrepreneurs, our focus is our most valuable asset. It allows us to stay focused on the tasks at hand and make the most of every opportunity." In the fast-paced world of entrepreneurship, it can be easy to get sidetracked. Staying focused requires a strong sense of purpose and the ability to stay focused on the bigger picture. Throughout my entrepreneurship journey there were always obstacles that kept me away from my focus almost on a daily basis. Staying focused was hard and required self discipline and dedication. It means setting aside distractions and staying committed to our vision, even when the road ahead is challenging. What I have learned through the years is in order to achieve success, we must stay focused on our goals and not get sidetracked by distractions or other obligations. This means staying organised and prioritising your tasks, and not letting yourself get overwhelmed by outside influences. Identify your goals and prioritise them. Having clear goals can help you stay focused on what's most important. Take some time to think about what you want to achieve, both in your work and personal life, and make a plan for how you will achieve those goals.

Create a conducive environment. Your surroundings can have a big impact on your ability to focus. Make sure your workspace is clean, organised, and free from distractions. If you work from home, try to create a dedicated work area that is separate from your living space.

Set boundaries. It's important to set boundaries with yourself and others to protect your time and focus. For example, you can turn off notifications on your phone, or let your coworkers know that you need some time to focus on a task.

Minimise multitasking. Research has shown that multitasking can actually decrease your productivity and focus. Instead of trying to do multiple things at once, focus on one task at a time and give it your full attention.

Take regular breaks. Although it may seem counterintuitive, taking regular breaks can actually help you stay focused. Taking a short break every hour or so can help you recharge and refocus your attention. Exercise and eat well. Taking care of your physical health can also improve your mental focus. Make sure to get regular exercise and eat a healthy, balanced diet. This can help you stay energised and alert throughout the day.

Get enough sleep. Sleep is essential for maintaining focus and concentration. Make sure you're getting enough sleep at night, and try to establish a regular sleep schedule.

Practice mindfulness. Mindfulness is the practice of focusing on the present moment, without judgement. This can help you stay focused and calm, even in the face of distractions. There are many different mindfulness techniques you can try, such as meditation or deep breathing.

Use techniques to increase focus. There are many techniques you can use to help you focus, such as the Pomodoro Technique or the 50/10 rule. These techniques involve breaking up your work into smaller, manageable chunks and taking regular breaks in between.

Seek help if needed. If you're having trouble staying focused, it may be helpful to seek support from others. This could include talking to a therapist, joining a support group, or working with a coach or mentor. Be patient and persistent. Finally, remember that developing focus and concentration takes time and practice. Don't be discouraged if you struggle at first — keep working at it and you will gradually improve.

Keep a to-do list. A to-do list can help you stay organised and focused by providing a clear overview of what you need to accomplish. Write down all of your tasks and priorities, and check them off as you complete them. This can help you stay on track and avoid getting overwhelmed.

Eliminate distractions. Distractions can be a major obstacle to focus, so it's important to eliminate them as much as possible. This could include turning off notifications on your phone or computer, closing unnecessary tabs on your web browser, or working in a quiet environment.

Use white noise. White noise can help you focus by blocking out other sounds and distractions. There are many white noise apps and websites available, or you can try using a white noise machine or listening to soothing music. Take care of your mental health. Mental health is an important factor in maintaining focus and concentration. Make sure to take care of yourself by practising self-care, setting aside time for relaxation and leisure activities, and seeking help if needed. Use technology to your advantage. Technology can be both a help and a hindrance to focus. While it can provide useful tools and resources, it can also be a major source of distractions. Use technology wisely by using tools like productivity apps or website blockers to stay focused and avoid getting sidetracked.

Avoid procrastination. Procrastination can be a major obstacle to focus, as it can lead to last-minute rushes and stress. Avoid procrastination by setting aside dedicated time for tasks and prioritising your to-do list. Manage your time effectively. Time management is an important skill for maintaining focus and productivity. Create a schedule for yourself and stick to it, breaking up your tasks into manageable chunks and allowing yourself regular breaks. Stay motivated.

Motivation is key to staying focused and engaged in your work and life. Find ways to stay motivated, such as setting challenging but achievable goals, rewarding yourself for your accomplishments, and staying positive and optimistic.

Remember to have fun. Finally, don't forget to have fun and enjoy yourself! Staying focused and productive doesn't have to be all work and no play. Make sure to find time for activities and hobbies that you enjoy, and remember to take breaks and relax. In conclusion, staying focused in work and life requires a combination of planning, self-care, and persistence. By setting clear goals, creating a conducive environment, minimising distractions, and practising mindfulness and other focus-enhancing techniques, you can improve your ability to concentrate and achieve your goals.

The tenth degree is being proactive.

"Proactivity requires a proactive mindset. It means being proactive in seeking out opportunities and being proactive in solving problems."

"Proactivity is a choice. It requires us to be proactive in our thinking and proactive in our actions." Being proactive is about taking ownership of our own lives and not waiting for things to happen to us. It's about being proactive in making things happen. Instead of waiting for opportunities to come to me, I took the initiative and created them by following this plan outlined in my book. This means being proactive in your approach and seeking out new challenges and opportunities to grow and learn.

Identify your goals and priorities. Before you can be proactive, you need to know what you want to achieve. Take some time to think about your long-term and short-term goals, and what is most important to you.

Take control of your time. Proactive people are good at managing their time and making the most of every day. Start by creating a daily schedule and sticking to it.

Anticipate problems and develop solutions. Proactive people don't just react to problems as they arise; they anticipate potential issues and plan for them in advance.

This means taking the time to think about what could go wrong and coming up with strategies to prevent or mitigate any negative effects.

Take initiative and be willing to act. Being proactive means going beyond just reacting to situations and taking the initiative to make things happen. This might mean speaking up in a meeting, making a suggestion to your boss, or volunteering for a new project.

Take responsibility for your actions. Proactive people take ownership of their actions and the outcomes of those actions. This means being willing to admit when you've made a mistake and taking steps to correct it, rather than trying to blame someone else.

Be adaptable and open to change. Proactive people are flexible and willing to adapt to changing circumstances. They are open to new ideas and willing to try new things, even if it means stepping out of their comfort zone. Seek out opportunities and challenges. Proactive people are always on the lookout for opportunities to learn, grow, and develop. This might mean taking on new projects, pursuing new hobbies, or learning new skills. Be persistent and resilient. Proactive people don't give up easily. They are willing to work hard and put in the effort to achieve their goals, even when faced with setbacks or challenges.

Communicate effectively. Proactive people are good at communicating with others, both verbally and in writing. They are able to clearly express their thoughts and ideas, and listen actively to others.

Build positive relationships. Proactive people know that their success is often dependent on the support and cooperation of others. They work to build positive relationships with their coworkers, bosses, and others, and are willing to help others in return.

Continuously improve and learn. Proactive people are always looking for ways to improve themselves and their work. They are open to feedback and willing to learn from their mistakes, and are constantly seeking out new opportunities for growth and development.

Set specific and measurable goals. Proactive people know that setting specific, measurable goals is essential for success. They take the time to define what they want to achieve, and create a plan for how they will reach their goals.

Take care of your physical and mental health. Being proactive requires a lot of energy and focus, and it's important to take care of your physical and mental health in order to be successful. This means getting regular exercise, eating a healthy diet, and making time for relaxation and self-care.

Be proactive in your personal life. Being proactive doesn't just apply to work; it's also important in your personal life. This means setting goals for your relationships, hobbies, and personal development, and taking steps to achieve those goals.

Stay organised and focused. Proactive people know that staying organised and focused is key to achieving their goals. They use tools like calendars, to-do lists, and planners to stay on track and make the most of their time.

Take calculated risks. Proactive people are willing to take calculated risks in pursuit of their goals. This means carefully weighing the potential risks and rewards of a decision, and then making an informed choice.

Be confident and assertive. Proactive people have confidence in themselves and their abilities, and are willing to assert themselves when necessary. This means speaking up for what you believe in, standing up for yourself, and being willing to take on challenging tasks.

Be positive and optimistic. Proactive people have a positive attitude and believe in their ability to succeed. They stay optimistic even when faced with setbacks or challenges, and use that optimism to fuel their drive and determination.

Continuously assess and adjust your approach. Proactive people are always looking for ways to improve their approach and strategies. They regularly assess their progress and make adjustments as needed to ensure they are on track to achieving their goals.

Be proactive in your career. Being proactive in your career means taking charge of your own development and career path. This might mean seeking out new opportunities, networking, and continuously learning and growing.

Lead by example. Proactive people are leaders in their own right, and they know that the best way to inspire others to be proactive is to lead by example. This means showing others what it means to be proactive, and setting a positive and inspiring example for others to follow. Embrace challenges and obstacles. Proactive people know that challenges and obstacles are inevitable, and they embrace them as opportunities to learn and grow. They view challenges as a natural part of the journey towards achieving their goals, and use them as motivation to keep moving forward.

Invest in your personal and professional development. Proactive people know that continuous learning and growth is essential for success. They invest in their personal and professional development by seeking out opportunities for learning, networking, and improving their skills and abilities.

Collaborate and build partnerships. Proactive people know that they can't achieve their goals on their own, and they are willing to collaborate and build partnerships with others in order to succeed. This means seeking out opportunities to work with others, and being open to different perspectives and ideas.

Be proactive in your community. Being proactive doesn't just apply to your personal and professional life; it also applies to your community. This means taking an active role in making your community a better place, and working to create positive change and improve the lives of others.

Stay motivated and focused. Proactive people know that staying motivated and focused is essential for achieving their goals. They use a variety of techniques to stay motivated, such as setting rewards for themselves, breaking their goals down into smaller, more manageable tasks, and staying positive and optimistic.

Be proactive in your relationships. Being proactive in your relationships means taking an active role in making them strong and healthy. This might mean setting goals for your relationships, communicating openly and honestly with others, and being willing to work through conflicts and challenges.

Share your knowledge and experiences. Proactive people know that sharing their knowledge and experiences with others is an important part of their personal and professional growth.

They are willing to mentor others, share their expertise, and help others learn and grow. In conclusion, being proactive is an important mindset and skill that can help you achieve success in both your personal and professional life. It involves taking control of your time and actions, anticipating problems and developing solutions, and continuously learning and improving. By following the tips and strategies outlined in this book, you can develop a proactive mindset and start achieving your goals today.

The eleventh degree is being adaptable.

"Being adaptable requires an open and curious mindset. It means being willing to learn and grow, and to embrace new perspectives and experiences."

"Adaptability is a valuable skill in both personal and professional settings. It allows us to be flexible and adapt to new roles and responsibilities, and to find success in a variety of environments." Adaptability is a key characteristic of successful individuals. It allows us to adapt to new environments and conditions, and to be resilient in the face of challenges. Everytime I moved to a new state to start my ventures I always had to be adaptable. The world is constantly changing, and in order to be successful, we must be able to adapt and change with it. This means being open to new ideas and approaches, and being willing to try new things.

Be open-minded. To be adaptable, it's important to be open-minded and willing to consider new ideas and perspectives. Don't be afraid to challenge your assumptions and be receptive to feedback and criticism.

Be flexible. Being adaptable means being able to change and adjust to different situations. Be open to trying new things and be willing to alter your plans or approach if needed.

Learn from your mistakes. Mistakes are a natural part of life and can provide valuable opportunities for learning and growth. Instead of getting discouraged by setbacks, use them as opportunities to learn and improve.

Embrace change. Change is a constant in life and in business, so it's important to be able to adapt to new situations and challenges. Instead of resisting change, embrace it and see it as an opportunity for growth and progress.

Stay positive. A positive attitude can go a long way in helping you adapt to new situations. Stay optimistic and look for the silver lining, even in difficult or challenging situations.

Be proactive. To be adaptable, you need to be proactive and take the initiative. Don't wait for things to happen – make them happen.

Be resilient. Resilience is the ability to bounce back from setbacks and challenges. Develop your resilience by practising self-care, setting goals, and seeking support when needed. Be willing to learn. To be adaptable, you need to be willing to learn and grow. Take advantage of opportunities to learn new skills and acquire new knowledge, whether through formal education or on-the-job training.

Be a team player. Adaptability is not just an individual trait – it's also a team trait. To be adaptable, you need to be able to work effectively with others and be a valuable member of the team.

Be willing to take risks. To be adaptable, you need to be willing to take calculated risks and step outside your comfort zone. This can be scary, but it's also where the greatest opportunities for growth and success lie.

Be persistent. Finally, remember that adaptability is a skill that takes time and practice to develop. Don't be discouraged if you struggle at first – keep working at it and you will gradually improve.
Develop a growth mindset. A growth mindset is the belief that you can grow and develop through effort and learning. This mindset is crucial for adaptability, as it allows you to approach challenges and setbacks as opportunities for growth and improvement.
Be proactive in seeking feedback. Feedback is an essential tool for learning and growth, but it's not always easy to receive. To be adaptable, you need to be proactive in seeking out feedback and be open to hearing constructive criticism. Be solution-focused. To be adaptable, you need to be solution-focused rather than problem-focused. This means looking for ways to overcome challenges and obstacles, rather than getting bogged down in the problems themselves.

Be resourceful. Resourcefulness is an important trait for adaptability. Be creative and resourceful in finding solutions to challenges, and be willing to think outside the box.

Be resilient in the face of failure. Failure is a natural part of life and business, and it's important to be resilient in the face of failure. Don't be discouraged by setbacks – instead, learn from them and use them as opportunities for growth and improvement.

Stay curious. Curiosity is a key trait for adaptability, as it allows you to learn and grow from new experiences and challenges. Keep your curiosity alive by seeking out new experiences and learning opportunities.

Embrace diversity. Diversity brings a wide range of perspectives and experiences to the table, and it's important to be adaptable to different perspectives and backgrounds. Embrace diversity and be open to learning from others.

Be adaptable in your communication. To be adaptable, you need to be able to adapt your communication style to different situations and audiences. Be aware of the context and the needs of your audience, and adjust your communication accordingly.

Be adaptable in your leadership style. Adaptability is also important in leadership. As a leader, you need to be able to adapt your leadership style to different situations and challenges. Be flexible and responsive, and be willing to adjust your approach as needed.

Be adaptable in your work style. To be adaptable, you need to be able to adapt your work style to different tasks and projects. Be flexible and willing to try new approaches, and be open to feedback and suggestions from others.
Be adaptable in your thinking. Adaptability also requires being open to new ideas and ways of thinking. Be willing to challenge your assumptions and beliefs, and be receptive to different perspectives and viewpoints.

Be adaptable in your decision-making. To be adaptable, you need to be able to make good decisions in a variety of situations. Be open to new information and consider different options before making a decision.

Be adaptable in your problem-solving. Problem-solving is an essential skill for adaptability, as it allows you to find solutions to a wide range of challenges and obstacles. Be creative and resourceful in your problem-solving, and be willing to try different approaches.

Be adaptable in your time management. Time management is another key skill for adaptability, as it allows you to be flexible and respond to changing priorities and deadlines. Be organised and efficient in your time management, and be willing to adjust your schedule as needed.

Be adaptable in your relationships. Adaptability is also important in your personal and professional relationships. Be open to new relationships and be willing to adapt to the needs and preferences of others.

Be adaptable in your personal growth. Finally, remember that adaptability is not just a business trait – it's also a personal trait. Be open to new experiences and challenges in your personal life, and be willing to adapt and grow as a person.

In conclusion, being adaptable is a valuable skill in both business and life. It involves being open-minded, flexible, and solution-focused, and it requires a willingness to learn and grow. Adaptability also requires being proactive, resilient, and resourceful, and being able to adapt to different situations and challenges. By developing these skills and traits, you can become more adaptable and better able to succeed in a changing world. Being adaptable allows us to be agile and responsive to change, and to thrive in constantly evolving environments.

The twelfth degree is being resilient.

"Resilience is not about being immune to adversity, but about being able to bounce back from it. It's about having the resilience to keep going, no matter what life throws our way."

"Resilience is a key factor in achieving success. It allows us to persevere through challenges and setbacks, and to emerge stronger and more resilient as a result." Resilience is the ability to bounce back from adversity and continue moving forward. When I lost almost a fortune to bad investments in the past, I didn't give up and moved on. I took time to reevaluate the situation and find a solution to move forward with better choices and more rewarding aspects of it. The situation was about being able to overcome challenges and setbacks, and to persevere through tough times. Success often requires overcoming challenges and obstacles, and it is important to be resilient and bounce back from these setbacks. This means staying positive and not letting setbacks discourage you from achieving your goals.

Develop a positive mindset: Having a positive mindset can help you approach challenges and difficult situations with optimism and resilience. This can involve reframing negative thoughts, practising gratitude, and focusing on the good things in your life.

Set goals and work towards them: Setting goals can provide direction and motivation, and working towards them can give a sense of accomplishment and progress. This can help you stay resilient and continue moving forward, even in the face of setbacks.

Learn from failures and setbacks: It's important to view failures and setbacks as opportunities for growth and learning. Instead of getting discouraged, try to identify the causes of the failure and what you can do differently in the future. This can help you develop resilience and bounce back from challenges. Build strong relationships: Strong relationships with friends, family, and colleagues can provide support and encouragement during difficult times. Having people to talk to and confide in can help you cope with stress and challenges, and can also provide a sense of belonging and connection. Take care of your physical and mental health: Your physical and mental health are closely connected, and taking care of both is essential for resilience. This can involve exercising regularly, eating a healthy diet, getting enough sleep, and practising stress-management techniques like meditation or deep breathing. Develop a growth mindset: Having a growth mindset means believing that your abilities and skills can be developed through effort and practice. This can help you approach challenges with a sense of determination and perseverance, and can also help you bounce back from setbacks and failures.

Stay adaptable and flexible: Resilient people are able to adapt to change and handle unexpected challenges. This can involve being open to new ideas and approaches, and being willing to try different strategies to overcome obstacles.

Practice self-compassion: Being hard on yourself can make it difficult to bounce back from setbacks and failures. Instead, try to be kind and understanding towards yourself, and remind yourself that everyone makes mistakes and faces challenges. This can help you develop resilience and move forward.

Develop a sense of purpose and meaning: Having a sense of purpose and meaning in your work and life can provide motivation and direction, and can also help you cope with challenges and setbacks. This can involve identifying your values and goals, and finding ways to align your actions with them.

Seek support and help when needed: Resilient people know when to ask for help and support, and are not afraid to seek assistance when needed. This can involve reaching out to friends, family, or a therapist for emotional support, or seeking advice from mentors or colleagues on how to overcome challenges.

Keep a positive attitude and perspective: Having a positive attitude and perspective can help you stay resilient and optimistic, even in the face of adversity.

This can involve focusing on the good things in your life, finding humour in difficult situations, and staying hopeful for the future.

Build and maintain a support network: Building a network of supportive people can provide valuable resources and assistance when facing challenges. This can involve cultivating relationships with friends, family, and colleagues, and seeking out mentors and other individuals who can offer guidance and advice.

Learn from successful individuals: Resilient people often look to others who have overcome adversity and achieved success for inspiration and guidance. This can involve reading biographies of successful individuals, attending workshops or seminars, or seeking out mentorship opportunities to learn from others who have faced and overcome challenges.

Prioritise self-care: Taking care of yourself is essential for maintaining resilience. This can involve engaging in activities that nourish your mind, body, and spirit, such as exercising, meditating, or pursuing hobbies that bring you joy. Develop effective coping skills: Resilient individuals have a range of coping skills that they can use to manage stress and challenges. This can involve practising mindfulness, setting realistic goals, and seeking out healthy outlets for stress, such as exercise or creative expression.

Embrace change: Change is a constant in life, and resilient individuals are able to adapt and respond to change with flexibility and grace. This can involve being open to new experiences and perspectives, and being willing to let go of old ways of doing things in favour of more effective approaches.

Stay focused and persistent: Resilient individuals are able to stay focused and persistent, even in the face of setbacks or obstacles. This can involve setting clear goals and developing a plan to achieve them, and staying committed to your goals even when things get difficult. Practice gratitude: Cultivating a sense of gratitude can help you maintain a positive attitude and perspective, even in the face of adversity. This can involve taking time each day to reflect on the things that you are grateful for, and expressing your gratitude to others. Seek out new experiences and challenges: Resilient individuals are not afraid to step outside their comfort zone and try new things. This can involve seeking out new experiences and challenges, and being willing to take risks and learn from your mistakes. Maintain a healthy work-life balance: Balancing the demands of work and personal life can be challenging, but it is essential for maintaining resilience. This can involve setting boundaries and prioritising your physical and mental health, and making time for the things that bring you joy and fulfilment outside of work.

Find ways to give back: Helping others and making a positive impact in the world can provide a sense of purpose and fulfilment, and can also help build resilience. This can involve volunteering for a cause you care about, or finding ways to support and assist others in your community.

In conclusion, resilience is an important quality that can help individuals navigate challenges and adversity in work and life. There are many strategies and approaches that can help individuals develop resilience, including developing a positive mindset, setting goals and working towards them, learning from failures and setbacks, building strong relationships, taking care of physical and mental health, and practising self-compassion.

In order to be resilient, it's important to have a positive attitude and to focus on the things we can control. This helps us to stay focused and motivated, even in the face of adversity.

By implementing these strategies, individuals can build their resilience and be better equipped to handle the challenges and difficulties that life may throw their way.

The thirteenth degree is being creative.

"Creativity is a limitless resource. It allows us to tap into our own potential and to find new and innovative ways to express ourselves and make a positive impact on the world."

"Being creative means thinking outside the box and coming up with new and innovative ideas. It's about using our imagination and taking risks to find unique solutions to problems" Being creative requires an open and curious mindset. When I opened my first restaurant during the US housing crises I only had a set amount of money and had to be creative to be able to open it with limited resources at hand. It meant being open to new experiences and perspectives, and being willing to try new things like only being open for limited hours to save on other costs and increase profitability. Success often requires thinking outside the box and coming up with creative solutions to problems. This means being open to new ideas and approaches, and not being afraid to try something different. These are the steps that have helped me become more creative.

Before you can start being creative, you need to define what you want to achieve. Whether it's a project at work or a personal goal in your life, having a clear idea of what you want to accomplish will help you stay focused and motivated.

To be creative, you need a space where you can think and work without distractions. This could be a dedicated room in your home, a quiet corner of your office, or even a favourite coffee shop. The important thing is to find a place where you feel comfortable and can focus on your work.

Creativity often comes from a relaxed and open mind. To get into this state, try taking some time to meditate or do some light exercise before you start working. This will help you clear your head and focus on the task at hand.

To be truly creative, you need to be willing to take risks and try new things. This means stepping outside of your comfort zone and trying things that may be a little scary or uncomfortable. It's okay to fail – in fact, failure is often a necessary step on the path to success.

No one else has your unique perspective and experiences, so don't be afraid to let your own voice shine through in your work. This will make your ideas more interesting and original, and help you stand out from the crowd. Creativity is often a team effort, so don't be afraid to reach out to others for help or input. Whether it's a colleague at work or a friend in your personal life, surrounding yourself with supportive and creative people can help you come up with even better ideas.

Ideas can strike at any time, so it's important to have a way to capture them when they do. Keep a small notebook or use a note-taking app on your phone to jot down your thoughts and ideas as they come to you. This will not only help you stay organised, but it can also provide inspiration for future projects.

Creativity often thrives when you're well-rested and refreshed, so make sure to take breaks throughout the day. This could mean going for a walk, listening to some music, or simply taking a few minutes to clear your head. Taking regular breaks will help you stay energised and focused on your work.

Like any skill, creativity requires practice to develop and improve. Make sure to set aside time on a regular basis to work on creative projects, even if they're just for fun. This will help you stay sharp and keep your ideas flowing. Creativity often comes from trying new things and seeing what works. So don't be afraid to experiment with different techniques, materials, or approaches. This will not only help you develop your skills, but it can also lead to unexpected and exciting results. Creativity is a journey, not a destination. Even when you hit a roadblock or face a setback, keep pushing forward. With practice and persistence, you can develop your creativity and use it to achieve your goals in work and life.

To be creative, you need to stay curious and open to new ideas. This means always being on the lookout for new information and experiences, and being willing to learn from others. This can help you stay fresh and inspire new ideas for your work.

Creativity often comes from pushing yourself to think in new and different ways. This could mean trying a new creative technique, working on a more ambitious project, or simply trying to see things from a different perspective. By challenging yourself, you can break out of your comfort zone and unlock your full creative potential.

To be truly creative, you need to be able to step back and reflect on your work. This means taking the time to review what you've done, and think about what worked and what didn't. This will help you identify areas for improvement, and give you a better sense of where you want to go next.

Creativity is not a straight path to success – there will be setbacks and failures along the way. But instead of seeing these as failures, try to see them as opportunities to learn and grow. By embracing failure and using it as a source of feedback, you can improve your work and become more creative.

Getting feedback from others can be a great way to improve your work and develop your creativity. This could mean asking a colleague for their thoughts on a project, or sharing your work with a friend or mentor for their input. By seeking feedback, you can gain new perspectives and insights that can help you take your work to the next level.

To be truly creative, you need to be willing to take risks and try new things. This means stepping outside of your comfort zone and trying things that may be a little scary or uncomfortable. It's okay to fail – in fact, failure is often a necessary step on the path to success.

Creativity often comes from being open to new ideas and experiences. This means being willing to listen to others and consider different perspectives, even if they're different from your own. By being open to new ideas, you can expand your horizons and come up with more original and interesting work.

Creativity is all about using your imagination to come up with new and interesting ideas. This means letting your mind wander and exploring different possibilities, even if they seem a little far-fetched at first. By using your imagination, you can come up with ideas that are truly unique and original.

To be creative, you need to keep learning and growing. This means staying up to date with the latest developments in your field, and always being on the lookout for new information and experiences. By continuing to learn, you can keep your mind sharp and open to new ideas.

Creativity is a journey, and it's important to celebrate your successes along the way. Whether it's completing a challenging project, trying a new creative technique, or simply coming up with a great idea, take the time to celebrate your achievements. This will help you stay motivated and inspired, and keep you moving forward on your creative journey. To be creative, it can be helpful to have a supportive community of like-minded people around you. This could mean joining a local creative group, attending workshops or classes, or simply connecting with other creative individuals online. By building a network of supportive and inspiring people, you can gain valuable insights and feedback that can help you improve your work. To be truly creative, you need to take care of yourself and make sure you're well-rested and energised. This means setting aside time for self-care and relaxation, and making sure you get enough sleep, exercise, and healthy food. By taking care of yourself, you can keep your mind and body in top condition and be ready to tackle any creative challenge that comes your way.

Creativity can be a roller coaster ride, with moments of exhilaration and excitement followed by periods of doubt and frustration. To stay creative, it's important to maintain a positive attitude and stay focused on your goals. This means keeping a sense of humour, staying optimistic, and not letting setbacks or failures get you down.

Creativity is a journey, not a destination. Even when you hit a roadblock or face a setback, keep pushing forward. With practice and persistence, you can develop your creativity and use it to achieve your goals in work and life. Don't give up, and keep moving forward – the best is yet to come! In conclusion, being creative at work and in life requires a combination of focus, persistence, and a willingness to take risks.

By defining your goals, finding your creative space, and staying curious and open to new ideas, you can unlock your full creative potential and use it to achieve your goals. Remember to take care of yourself, seek feedback and support, and keep pushing forward – with dedication and effort, you can become a truly creative individual.

The fourteenth degree is being passionate.

"Passion is the fuel that drives us forward. It gives us the energy and motivation to keep going, even when the road ahead is challenging."

"Being passionate means being driven and motivated by a deep sense of purpose and meaning. It's about being passionate about something and pursuing it with excitement and determination" Passion is a powerful force. It allows us to pursue our dreams and to make a positive impact on the world. Developing passion is a highly individualised process, as what sparks passion in one person may not do the same for another. Remember, developing passion takes time and effort, and it is not something that will happen overnight. Be patient with yourself and keep working at it, and you will eventually find something that truly sparks your passion. "Passion is contagious. When we are passionate about something, it inspires others to be passionate as well."

Identify your interests and passions. Take some time to think about the things that truly excite and motivate you. These could be activities, hobbies, causes, or anything else that brings you joy and fulfilment. "Passion is a powerful force. It allows us to pursue our dreams and to make a positive impact on the world."

Set specific goals for yourself. Having clear goals can help you focus and stay motivated as you work towards becoming more passionate in your work and life. These goals should be challenging, but also achievable and aligned with your interests and passions.

Take on new challenges and experiences. Passion often comes from a sense of growth and accomplishment. Challenge yourself by trying new things, learning new skills, and taking on new responsibilities. This will help you expand your horizons and discover new passions.

Surround yourself with passionate people. Being around others who are passionate about their work and life can be contagious. Seek out people who inspire and motivate you, and learn from their experiences and advice.

Find ways to connect your work and life with your passions. One of the keys to becoming more passionate is to find ways to integrate your interests and passions into your work and daily activities. This could mean pursuing a career that aligns with your passions, volunteering for causes you care about, or simply finding ways to incorporate your interests into your everyday life.
Practice mindfulness and gratitude. Mindfulness and gratitude are powerful tools for increasing passion and enjoyment in life.

By being present in the moment and appreciating what you have, you can foster a deeper sense of fulfilment and joy. Take care of yourself. Being passionate and engaged in your work and life requires energy and focus. Make sure to prioritise your physical and mental health by getting enough sleep, exercise, and healthy food. This will help you maintain the energy and focus you need to pursue your passions.

Create a supportive environment. Your environment can have a big impact on your level of passion and engagement. Create a workspace and living space that is conducive to productivity and enjoyment. This could mean decluttering, organising, and adding personal touches that inspire and motivate you. Cultivate a positive mindset. A positive mindset can make a big difference in your level of passion and engagement. Practise positive self-talk, focus on the good things in your life, and let go of negative thoughts and emotions that hold you back.

Take time for yourself. It can be easy to get caught up in the hustle and bustle of daily life, but it's important to make time for yourself. Take regular breaks, indulge in your hobbies and interests, and do things that bring you joy and relaxation. This will help you recharge and stay passionate and engaged.

Keep learning and growing. Passion often comes from a sense of growth and progress. Make sure to continue learning and expanding your skills and knowledge. This could mean taking classes, attending workshops, or simply reading and staying up-to-date on your industry or interests.

Get out of your comfort zone. Passion often comes from pushing yourself outside of your comfort zone and trying new things. Don't be afraid to take risks and try things that scare you. This will help you grow, learn, and discover new passions.

Take responsibility for your actions. Being passionate and engaged in your work and life requires taking ownership and responsibility for your actions. Take the time to reflect on your choices and decisions, and make sure they align with your passions and goals.

Stay organised and focused. Passion and engagement require focus and organisation. Make sure to prioritise your tasks, set deadlines, and create a schedule that allows you to accomplish your goals and pursue your passions.
Don't be afraid to fail. Failure is a natural part of the learning and growth process, and it can often lead to new discoveries and passions. Don't let fear of failure hold you back from pursuing your dreams and goals. Find ways to stay motivated and inspired.

Passion and engagement can sometimes wane, especially when faced with challenges and setbacks. To keep yourself motivated and inspired, seek out new experiences, surround yourself with passionate people, and find sources of inspiration, such as books, podcasts, or art. Practice self-care and self-compassion. Being passionate and engaged in your work and life requires taking care of yourself and treating yourself with kindness and compassion. Make sure to prioritise your physical and mental health, and don't be too hard on yourself when things don't go as planned. Connect with your community. Passion and engagement are often strengthened by a sense of connection and belonging. Find ways to connect with your community, whether that's through volunteering, joining a club or organisation, or simply spending time with friends and loved ones. Celebrate your successes and accomplishments. Passion and engagement are often fueled by a sense of accomplishment and recognition. Make sure to celebrate your successes and accomplishments, no matter how small they may seem. This will help you stay motivated and continue pursuing your passions. Keep striving for growth and improvement. Passion and engagement are ongoing journeys, not destinations. Keep striving for growth and improvement, and never stop pursuing your interests and passions. This will help you lead a fulfilling and joyful life.

Be open to change and adaptability. The world is constantly changing, and to stay passionate and engaged in your work and life, it's important to be open to change and adaptability. Embrace new opportunities, challenges, and experiences, and be willing to adapt and grow as needed.

Take time to reflect on your progress and accomplishments. Regular self-reflection is key to staying passionate and engaged in your work and life. Take time to reflect on your progress, challenges, and accomplishments, and use this information to set new goals and continue pursuing your passions. Find ways to give back and make a positive impact. Passion and engagement are often fueled by a sense of purpose and contribution. Find ways to give back and make a positive impact in your community, whether that's through volunteering, donating to a cause you care about, or simply helping others in need.

Stay true to your values and beliefs. Passion and engagement require alignment with your core values and beliefs. Make sure to stay true to what matters most to you, and let your passions and interests be guided by your values and principles. "Being passionate means being fully engaged and invested in what we do. It's about being passionate about something and pursuing it with all of our heart and soul."

Don't be afraid to ask for help and support. Pursuing your passions and staying engaged in your work and life can be challenging, and it's okay to ask for help and support when needed. Reach out to friends, family, mentors, or professionals for advice, guidance, and support. Find ways to incorporate mindfulness and relaxation into your daily routine. Mindfulness and relaxation are essential for maintaining passion and engagement. Keep an open mind and a positive attitude. Passion and engagement require an open mind and a positive attitude. Don't be afraid to try new things, learn from others, and embrace change. This will help you stay curious, open, and engaged in your work and life. Be persistent and consistent in pursuing your passions. Passion and engagement require persistence and consistency. Don't give up on your passions and interests, even when faced with challenges and setbacks. Keep working towards your goals, and never stop striving for growth and improvement. Celebrate and appreciate the small things. Passion and engagement are often fueled by a sense of gratitude and appreciation. Take the time to celebrate and appreciate the small things in life, such as the beauty of nature, the kindness of others, and the joy of simple pleasures. "Creativity is a key factor in personal and professional growth. It allows us to see things from new angles and to find new ways of solving problems." This will help you stay passionate and engaged in your work and life.

The fifteenth degree is being flexible.

"Flexibility is a valuable skill in both personal and professional settings. It allows us to be open to new experiences and opportunities, and to find success in a variety of environments."

Being flexible requires an open and adaptable mindset. It means being willing to consider new perspectives and approaches, and to adjust our plans as needed. Success often requires being flexible and adaptable in your approach. Being flexible means being open to change and adapting to new situations. It's about being able to roll with the punches and be agile in the face of change. After the US housing collapse, I could find any work so it was then when I started my own restaurant even though I didn't have much experience but I was determined to be able to provide for my family and go beyond my comfort zone and take a big risk. Being flexible meant being open to change and adapting to new situations. It's about being able to roll with the punches and be agile in the face of change. I started by setting specific, measurable, attainable, relevant, and time-bound goals for myself related to flexibility. For example, you might set a goal to work from home one day per week, or to be able to touch your toes by the end of the month.

Make a plan for how you will achieve your goals. This might involve creating a schedule for yourself, setting aside time for stretching and exercise, and finding ways to incorporate more flexibility into your daily routine.

Practice mindfulness and relaxation techniques to help you stay focused and calm, even in the face of challenges and setbacks. This can include things like meditation, deep breathing, or progressive muscle relaxation.

Prioritise physical fitness and flexibility by incorporating regular exercise into your routine. This could be as simple as going for a walk or jog, or taking a yoga or dance class.

Stay organised and on top of your workload by using tools and techniques like time management, task tracking, and goal setting. This can help you stay flexible and adaptable, even when things get busy or hectic.

Stay open-minded and be willing to try new things, even if they are outside of your comfort zone. This can help you stay flexible and adaptable, and can also lead to new opportunities and growth.

Collaborate and communicate with others to share ideas, solve problems, and find creative solutions. This can help you stay flexible and adaptable in your work and in your personal life. Take care of yourself by getting enough sleep, eating well, and managing stress. This can help you stay focused, energised, and able to handle whatever challenges come your way. Be proactive and take control of your own development. This might involve setting aside time for learning and skill-building, seeking out feedback and support from others, and taking on new challenges and opportunities.

Keep a positive attitude and focus on the things that you can control, rather than getting bogged down by stress and negativity. This can help you stay flexible and adaptable, and can also help you stay motivated and engaged.

Stay connected and engaged with others in your field, whether through networking events, professional organisations, or online communities. This can help you stay up-to-date on trends and developments, and can also provide valuable support and resources.

Be willing to take risks and try new things, even if they don't always work out. This can help you stay flexible and adaptable, and can also lead to new opportunities and growth.

Seek out feedback and support from others, whether through mentors, peers, or colleagues. This can help you stay on track and make sure that you are meeting your goals, and can also provide valuable insights and perspective.

Stay open to new ideas and perspectives, and be willing to adapt and change when necessary. This can help you stay flexible and adaptable, and can also lead to new opportunities and growth.

Practice self-care and prioritise your physical, mental, and emotional well-being. This can help you stay focused, energised, and able to handle whatever challenges come your way.

Be persistent and stay committed to your goals, even when things get tough or challenging. This can help you stay flexible and adaptable, and can also help you stay motivated and engaged.

Stay organised and on top of your workload by using tools and techniques like time management, task tracking, and goal setting. This can help you stay flexible and adaptable, even when things get busy or hectic.

Be proactive and take control of your own development. This might involve setting aside time for learning and skill-building, seeking out feedback and support from others, and taking on new challenges and opportunities.

Keep a positive attitude and focus on the things that you can control, rather than getting bogged down by stress and negativity. This can help you stay flexible and adaptable, and can also help you stay motivated and engaged.

Stay connected and engaged with others in your field, whether through networking events, professional organisations, or online communities. This can help you stay up-to-date on trends and developments, and can also provide valuable support and resources.

Be willing to take risks and try new things, even if they don't always work out. This can help you stay flexible and adaptable, and can also lead to new opportunities and growth.

Seek out feedback and support from others, whether through mentors, peers, or colleagues. This can help you stay on track and make sure that you are meeting your goals, and can also provide valuable insights and perspective.

Stay open to new ideas and perspectives, and be willing to adapt and change when necessary. This can help you stay flexible and adaptable, and can also lead to new opportunities and growth.

Keep a positive attitude and focus on the things that you can control, rather than getting bogged down by stress and negativity. This can help you stay flexible and adaptable, and can also help you stay motivated and engaged.

Be willing to take risks and try new things, even if they don't always work out. This can help you stay flexible and adaptable, and can also lead to new opportunities and growth.

Stay open to new ideas and perspectives, and be willing to adapt and change when necessary. This can help you stay flexible and adaptable, and can also lead to new opportunities and growth.

Be persistent and stay committed to your goals, even when things get tough or challenging. This can help you stay flexible and adaptable, and can also help you stay motivated and engaged.

Stay organised and on top of your workload by using tools and techniques like time management, task tracking, and goal setting. This can help you stay flexible and adaptable, even when things get busy or hectic.

Be proactive and take control of your own development. This might involve setting aside time for learning and skill-building, seeking out feedback and support from others, and taking on new challenges and opportunities. "In today's fast-paced world, being flexible is more important than ever. It allows us to be agile and responsive to change, and to thrive in constantly evolving environments."

In conclusion, becoming a flexible entrepreneur requires setting specific goals, making a plan to achieve those goals, practising mindfulness and relaxation techniques, prioritising physical fitness and flexibility, staying organised and on top of your workload, staying open-minded and willing to try new things, collaborating and communicating with others, taking care of yourself, being proactive and taking control of your own development, keeping a positive attitude, staying connected and engaged with others in your field, being willing to take risks and try new things, seeking out feedback and support from others, staying open to new ideas and perspectives, practising self-care, being persistent and committed to your goals, and staying organised and on top of your workload.

"Flexibility is a key characteristic of successful individuals. It allows us to be adaptable and responsive to new challenges and opportunities as they arise." By following these steps, you can become a flexible entrepreneur and be successful in both your work and personal life.

The sixteenth degree is being determined.

"Determination is a key factor in achieving success. It allows us to persevere through challenges and setbacks, and to emerge stronger and more determined as a result."

"To be determined, we must have a clear sense of purpose and the willingness to work hard to achieve our goals. It requires discipline and dedication to stay on track and make progress." Being determined means having the resilience to bounce back from adversity. It's about having the determination to keep going, no matter what life throws our way. I was always determined in my younger years to become the first millionaire in my family. It took me years but through following and developing my thirty degrees of success I finally became one. Determination is an important quality for hard work. This means having the resilience and persistence to keep going, even when things are tough. When you're determined to succeed, you're willing to put in the extra effort and make the necessary sacrifices to reach your goals. This determination can be a powerful force that helps you overcome obstacles and achieve success. Let's follow these steps to be more determined in whatever you are pursuing in life.

Set clear goals: Before you can become determined, you need to know what you're working towards. Take some time to think about what you want to achieve in your business and life, and then create specific, measurable, achievable, relevant, and time-bound (SMART) goals to help guide you.

Create a plan: Once you have your goals in mind, it's time to create a plan to achieve them. Break your goals down into smaller, more manageable tasks, and then create a timeline for completing each one. This will help you stay organised and motivated as you work towards your goals.

Take action: The most important step in becoming determined is to take action. Don't wait for the perfect moment or for everything to be just right – take the first step towards your goals today. Even small steps can add up and make a big difference over time.

Stay focused: It's easy to get sidetracked or lose motivation when working towards your goals. To stay determined, you need to stay focused on your priorities and avoid distractions. This may involve setting boundaries, saying no to non-essential tasks, or finding ways to eliminate distractions from your environment.

Cultivate a positive attitude: A positive attitude is key to determination.

When you have a positive outlook, you're more likely to stay motivated and persevere through challenges. Practice gratitude, stay optimistic, and focus on the good things in your life to cultivate a positive attitude.

Seek support: It's tough to go it alone, so don't be afraid to seek support when you need it. Surround yourself with people who are supportive and encouraging, and consider working with a mentor or coach who can help you stay on track.

Learn from setbacks: Setbacks are a natural part of the journey towards your goals. Instead of letting setbacks discourage you, use them as opportunities to learn and grow. Reflect on what went wrong, and use that knowledge to make better decisions in the future.

Stay motivated: Motivation is the driving force behind determination, so it's important to find ways to stay motivated even when things get tough.

This may involve setting rewards for yourself, finding ways to stay energised, or reminding yourself of why your goals are important to you.

Practice resilience: Resilience is the ability to bounce back from setbacks and failures, and it's an important quality for anyone looking to become determined. Practice resilience by learning to cope with challenges and setbacks in a healthy way, and by developing a growth mindset that allows you to see challenges as opportunities for learning and growth.

Manage your time effectively: Time management is an important aspect of determination, as it helps you stay organised and focused on your priorities. Create a schedule that allows you to make progress towards your goals, and be sure to allocate enough time for rest and relaxation to avoid burnout.

Stay organised: In addition to managing your time effectively, it's also important to stay organised to stay determined. This may involve creating a to-do list, keeping a calendar, or finding other ways to stay on top of tasks and commitments.

Take care of yourself: To stay determined, you need to take care of yourself physically, mentally, and emotionally. This includes getting enough sleep, eating a healthy diet, exercising regularly, and finding ways to manage stress and maintain your well-being.

Practice discipline: Discipline is the ability to follow through on your commitments and make consistent progress towards your goals. Practice discipline by setting and sticking to routines, avoiding procrastination, and being accountable for your actions.
Stay curious: Curiosity is an important quality for determination because it helps you stay engaged and motivated to learn and grow. Keep an open mind, ask questions, and seek out new experiences to stimulate your curiosity and keep you moving forward.

Learn from others: There are many successful people who have achieved great things through determination and hard work. Seek out role models and mentors who can share their experiences and insights with you, and learn from their successes and failures. Seek out challenges: While it's important to set realistic goals, it's also important to challenge yourself and push your limits. Seek out opportunities to test your skills and abilities, and be willing to take on new challenges as they arise. Stay humble: While determination is important, it's also important to stay humble and open to learning and growing. Recognize that you don't know everything, and be willing to seek out new experiences and insights to improve yourself and your business. Don't give up: Determination means never giving up, even when things get tough. Keep pushing through setbacks and challenges, and remind yourself of your goals and why they're important to you.

Celebrate your successes: It's important to celebrate your successes along the way, as this can help you stay motivated and determined. Take time to reflect on your progress, and be sure to reward yourself when you reach key milestones.

Stay adaptable: The business world is constantly changing, so it's important to stay adaptable and open to new ideas and approaches. Be willing to pivot and adjust your plans as needed, and stay open to learning new skills and techniques to stay ahead of the curve.

Believe in yourself: Finally, it's important to believe in

yourself and your abilities to become determined. Believe that you are capable of achieving your goals, and remind yourself of your past successes and strengths to build your confidence and determination.

Being determined is important for many reasons. It helps individuals to set goals for themselves and work towards achieving them, even when faced with challenges or obstacles. Determination allows individuals to persevere and persist in the face of adversity, which can ultimately lead to success.

In addition, determination can help individuals to maintain motivation and focus, which are key factors in achieving any goal. When faced with setbacks or challenges, determination can help individuals to stay on track and continue working towards their goals.

Furthermore, determination can have a positive impact on an individual's overall well-being and sense of satisfaction. By working towards and achieving goals, individuals can feel a sense of accomplishment and pride, which can boost self-esteem and confidence.

"Being determined means being focused and committed to achieving our goals. It's about having the determination to keep going, even when the road ahead is tough." In conclusion, determination is a valuable quality that can help individuals to achieve their goals and lead fulfilling, successful lives. It allows individuals to persevere and persist in the face of challenges and setbacks, and can ultimately lead to success, satisfaction, and well-being.

The seventeenth degree is being accountable.

"Accountability is not about perfection, it's about progress. It's about being willing to take risks, learn from our mistakes, and continually improve."

"Accountability is a critical aspect of any successful team or organisation. Without it, there is no trust, no accountability, and no progress." True accountability involves not only taking responsibility for our actions, but also actively striving to improve and do better in the future. To be truly accountable, we must be willing to own our mistakes and learn from them, rather than deflecting or denying them. When I made a negative investment or choice, I didn't blame anyone but myself, because I made that choice and I held myself accountable and learned from the mistake. In order to achieve success, you must be accountable for your actions and take responsibility for your mistakes. This means being honest with yourself and others, and being willing to admit when you are wrong. First we have to understand the concept of accountability. Before you can start becoming more accountable in business and life, it's important to understand what accountability means. Essentially, accountability means being responsible for your actions and decisions. It means accepting the consequences of your choices, both good and bad, and being willing to take ownership of them.

Set clear goals and expectations.One of the key ways to be more accountable is to set clear goals and expectations for yourself. This will help you to focus on what you need to do in order to be successful, and will also make it easier for others to hold you accountable.

Communicate openly and honestly. Effective communication is crucial for accountability. Make sure to be open and honest about your goals, your progress, and any challenges you may be facing. This will help others to understand where you stand and how they can support you.

Keep track of your progress.In order to be accountable, it's important to keep track of your progress and make sure you are on track to meet your goals. This could involve keeping a to-do list, setting deadlines, or using a project management tool to stay organised.

Take responsibility for your mistakes. Everyone makes mistakes from time to time, and it's important to take responsibility for them. This means acknowledging the mistake, apologising if necessary, and working to correct it. Seek feedback and support from friends, co-workers and family. In order to be accountable, it's important to be open to feedback and willing to ask for help when you need it. This could involve seeking feedback from colleagues, seeking guidance from a mentor, or joining a support group.

Set boundaries and manage your time effectively. In order to be accountable, it's important to set boundaries and manage your time effectively. This could involve setting limits on how much time you spend on certain tasks, delegating tasks to others, or saying no to requests that would stretch you too thin.

Learn from your past experiences. In order to be accountable, it's important to learn from your experiences and use them as opportunities for growth and development. This could involve reflecting on your successes and failures, seeking feedback from others, and seeking out new learning opportunities.

Practise self-awareness. Self-awareness is a key component of accountability. It involves being aware of your strengths and weaknesses, as well as how your actions and decisions impact others. Always hold yourself accountable to your values and beliefs. In order to be truly accountable, it's important to hold yourself accountable to your values and beliefs. This means making sure your actions and decisions align with your personal code of ethics. Seek out accountability partners. An accountability partner can be a valuable resource for helping you stay on track and achieve your goals. This could be a colleague, a mentor, or a friend who can help you stay focused and motivated.

Set specific, measurable, achievable, relevant, and time-bound (SMART) goals. In order to be more accountable, it's important to set specific, measurable, achievable, relevant, and time-bound (SMART) goals. This will help you to stay focused and motivated, and will make it easier for others to hold you accountable.

Use accountability software or tools. There are many software and tools available that can help you to be more accountable. These could include project management tools, time tracking software, or productivity apps. Develop a system for following up and checking in. In order to be more accountable, it's important to develop a system for following up and checking in on your progress. This could involve setting regular check-ins with yourself or others, setting reminders or alerts, or using a tracking system to monitor your progress. Seek out accountability training or resources. There are many resources available that can help you to develop your accountability skills. This could involve seeking out training or workshops, reading books or articles on the topic, or joining a group or community focused on accountability. Practise accountability in all areas of your life. Accountability isn't just important in business, it's also important in all areas of your life. This could include being accountable for your personal relationships, your health and wellness, and your financial responsibilities.

Foster a culture of accountability in your team or organisation. If you are a leader or manager, it's important to foster a culture of accountability within your team or organisation. This could involve setting clear expectations, providing support and resources, and holding others accountable for their actions and decisions.

Be open, honest, and transparent with your friends and loved ones, you can foster a sense of accountability and trust in your personal relationships. Accountability is also important in personal relationships. Encourage accountability in your relationships by setting clear expectations, communicating openly and honestly, and holding each other accountable for your actions and decisions.

Seek out accountability in your community. Accountability is important at all levels, including in your community. Seek out opportunities to be accountable in your community, whether through volunteering, participating in community projects, or advocating for change.

Continuously seek to improve your accountability skills. Accountability is a skill that can be developed and improved over time. Continuously seek out opportunities to improve your accountability skills, whether through training, feedback, or practice.

Be patient with yourself. Developing accountability skills takes time and effort, and it's important to be patient with yourself as you work to improve. Remember that setbacks and mistakes are a normal part of the learning process, and use them as opportunities to grow and learn. Accountability is important in both business and life because it helps to ensure that people take responsibility for their actions and decisions.

When individuals are accountable, they are more likely to take ownership of their work and to strive for excellence. This, in turn, leads to better performance and results, which can have a positive impact on the overall success of an organisation or individual. In addition to improving performance and results, accountability also fosters trust and credibility. When people are held accountable for their actions, they are more likely to be transparent and honest in their dealings with others. This helps to build trust and credibility, which are essential for building strong and productive relationships in both business and personal life.

The eighteenth degree is being open-minded.

"An open mind is like a parachute - it only works when it's open."

"An open mind is the key to unlocking new opportunities and experiences in life." True intelligence is the ability to hold multiple perspectives in your mind at once and still be open to more. Success often requires being open to new ideas and approaches, and not being afraid to try something different. This means being willing to listen to others and consider their perspectives, even if they are different from your own.

Understanding the concept of open-mindedness. Open-mindedness is the willingness to consider new ideas and perspectives, even if they differ from your own. It involves an openness to change, flexibility, and a willingness to learn and grow.

The importance of open-mindedness in business and life. Open-mindedness is crucial in both business and personal life as it allows us to adapt to new situations, solve problems, and make better decisions. It helps us to be more innovative, creative, and open to new opportunities.

How to cultivate open-mindedness. There are several ways to cultivate open-mindedness. Practising mindfulness and being present in the moment. Seeking out diverse perspectives and opinions. Being open to new experiences and trying new things. Asking questions and being curious about the world around you. Being willing to change your perspective or beliefs when presented with new information

The benefits of open-mindedness in business. Open-mindedness can lead to a number of benefits in business. Improved decision-making and problem-solving, Increased innovation and creativity. Better communication and collaboration with others and enhanced adaptability to change and flexibility.

The benefits of open-mindedness in personal life. Open-mindedness can also bring many benefits to our personal lives. Greater personal growth and development. Improved relationships with others. Enhanced empathy and understanding of others' perspectives. It also gives you greater life satisfaction and happiness.

Overcoming closed-mindedness. It is natural to have biases and preconceived notions, but it is important to recognize and try to overcome them in order to be open-minded. Some strategies for overcoming closed-mindedness. include Acknowledging your biases and seeking out diverse perspectives and opinions. Challenging your own beliefs and assumptions and being open to new experiences and trying new things.

The role of empathy in open-mindedness. Empathy, or the ability to understand and share the feelings of others, is closely linked to open-mindedness. By attempting to understand and see things from someone else's perspective, we can be more open to new ideas and viewpoints.

The importance of critical thinking in open-mindedness. Critical thinking, or the ability to analyse and evaluate information and arguments objectively, is also important for open-mindedness. By using critical thinking skills, we can more effectively consider and weigh different ideas and perspectives. The role of diversity in open-mindedness. Diversity, in terms of people and ideas, is important for open-mindedness as it exposes us to a range of perspectives and experiences. By seeking out diverse perspectives and experiences, we can broaden our thinking and be more open-minded. How to foster open-mindedness in the workplace. There are several ways that businesses can foster open-mindedness among their employees, including encouraging diversity and inclusion. Promoting a culture of questioning and curiosity. Providing opportunities for learning and growth. Encouraging open communication and the sharing of ideas.

The importance of open-mindedness in leadership. Open-mindedness is especially important for leaders as it allows them to effectively consider and weigh different perspectives, adapt to change, and make well-informed decisions.

Overcoming resistance to change. Change can be difficult, and it is natural to resist it. However, open-mindedness can help us to be more adaptable and open to change. Some strategies for overcoming resistance to change include recognizing and acknowledging our resistance. Understanding the reasons for the change and seeking out support and resources to help with the transition. Focusing on the potential benefits of the change.

The role of self-awareness in open-mindedness. Self-awareness, or the ability to recognize and understand our own thoughts, feelings, and behaviours, is important for open-mindedness as it allows us to identify and overcome our own biases and preconceived notions.

The importance of listening in open-mindedness. Listening is a crucial aspect of open-mindedness as it allows us to understand and consider the perspectives of others. By actively listening and engaging in open and honest communication, we can be more open to new ideas and viewpoints.

How to foster open-mindedness in personal relationships. Open-mindedness is important in personal relationships as it allows us to better understand and connect with others. Some ways to foster open-mindedness in personal relationships include, practising empathy and actively listening to others. Seeking out diverse perspectives and experiences. Being open to new experiences and trying new things together. Being open to change and trying new ways of interacting with each other

The role of humour in open-mindedness. Humour can be a useful tool for fostering open-mindedness as it helps to break down barriers and promotes a sense of openness and flexibility.

The importance of remaining open-minded in the face of criticism. It can be challenging to remain open-minded when faced with criticism, but it is important to try to consider the perspective of the person offering the criticism and use it as an opportunity for learning and growth.

The role of self-reflection in open-mindedness. Self-reflection, or the process of examining and evaluating our own thoughts, beliefs, and behaviours, can help us to identify and overcome biases and become more open-minded.

The importance of balance in open-mindedness. It is important to find a balance between being open to new ideas and maintaining our own beliefs and values. By considering and weighing different perspectives, we can find a balance between openness and conviction. Practising open-mindedness in daily life. Open-mindedness is a skill that can be cultivated and improved upon over time. By making a conscious effort to be open to new ideas and perspectives, and actively seeking out diverse experiences and perspectives, we can become more open-minded in our daily lives. Open-mindedness is a crucial skill that can bring many benefits to our personal and professional lives. It allows us to be more adaptable, innovative, and empathetic, and can lead to better decision-making, problem-solving, and relationships. As you have read there are many ways to cultivate open-mindedness, including practising mindfulness, seeking out diverse perspectives and experiences, and using critical thinking and self-reflection. "An open mind is a doorway to endless possibility and potential."

The most innovative and creative ideas come from those who are willing to embrace new and diverse perspectives."An open mind is a curious mind, and a curious mind is a mind that is always learning and growing." By actively working to be more open-minded, we can improve our personal and professional lives and create a more positive and understanding world.

The nineteenth degree is being a good communicator.

"Good communication involves not just the ability to express your own thoughts and feelings, but also the ability to truly listen and understand the perspectives of others."

"Effective communication involves more than just words – it also involves body language, tone, and the ability to read and respond to the emotions of others."
Good communication requires not only the ability to convey your message, but also the ability to truly understand and connect with the person you are speaking to. Success often requires being able to effectively communicate your ideas and thoughts to others. This means being able to listen to others and express yourself clearly and concisely. We become effective communicators through active listening. One of the most important skills for effective communication is the ability to actively listen to others. This means paying full attention to the speaker, maintaining eye contact, and avoiding distractions such as checking your phone or multitasking. It also means asking clarifying questions and expressing understanding of what the speaker is saying.
Communicate clearly and concisely. In both business and personal communication, it's important to be clear and concise in your messaging.

This means avoiding jargon and using language that is easy for others to understand. It also means being direct and getting to the point, rather than beating around the bush or using unnecessary filler words.

Use nonverbal cues effectively: Nonverbal cues, such as body language and facial expressions, can convey a lot of information. Make sure your nonverbal cues are in line with what you're trying to communicate. For example, if you're trying to show enthusiasm, make sure you're smiling and maintaining eye contact. If you're trying to convey confidence, stand up straight and make sure your posture is open and relaxed.

Be aware of your tone, the tone of your voice can greatly impact the way your message is received. Make sure you're aware of the tone you're using and that it's appropriate for the situation. For example, if you're giving a presentation, you'll want to use a confident and assertive tone. If you're having a difficult conversation with a colleague, you'll want to use a more empathetic and understanding tone.

Use assertive communication: Assertive communication is the ability to express your own thoughts, feelings, and needs in an open and honest way, while also respecting the thoughts, feelings, and needs of others. This means being able to speak up for yourself and say what you mean, without being aggressive or passive-aggressive. It also means being able to set boundaries and say no when necessary.

Always know your audience before you communicate, it's important to consider who your audience is and what they need to know.
This will help you tailor your message and choose the most effective medium for communication. For example, if you're communicating with a group of senior executives, you'll want to use a more formal and professional tone.
If you're communicating with a group of friends, a more casual and friendly tone may be more appropriate.

Use appropriate mediums for communication, such as email, phone, in-person meetings, and video conferencing. It's important to choose the most appropriate medium for the situation. For example, if you need to have a difficult conversation with a colleague, it may be better to do it in person rather than over email. If you need to communicate with a large group of people quickly, an email or group message may be more efficient.

Emphasise the benefits to your audience when you're communicating a message, it's important to focus on the benefits to your audience. This will help them see the value in what you're saying and be more likely to take action. For example, if you're trying to persuade a client to work with you, focus on how your product or service will solve their problems or improve their lives.

Use the powerful tool of storytelling for engaging your audience and making your message more memorable. Consider using stories to illustrate your points or to help your audience relate to what you're saying. Effective communication is a two-way street, so it's important to seek feedback and be open to criticism.

Practice empathy, which is the ability to understand and share the feelings of others. In order to effectively communicate with others, it's important to be able to put yourself in their shoes and try to see things from their perspective. This will help you better understand their needs and concerns, and it will also make them feel heard and valued.

Use positive language. The language you use can greatly impact the way your message is received. Make sure to use positive language, rather than negative language, whenever possible. This means focusing on what you can do or what you have, rather than what you can't do or what you don't have. For example, instead of saying "I can't do that," try saying "I'm not able to do that at this time, but here's what I can do instead."

Avoid misunderstandings by being specific in your communication. Make sure you're clear about what you mean and give enough context for others to understand. For example, if you're giving instructions, make sure you're specific about what needs to be done, when it needs to be done, and who is responsible for doing it.

Use inclusive language that is inclusive of all people, regardless of their gender, race, age, sexual orientation, or ability. In order to create a welcoming and inclusive environment, it's important to use language that is respectful and inclusive of everyone.

Using visual aids to support your message, such as charts, graphs, and images, can be very helpful in supporting your message and helping your audience understand and remember what you're saying. Make sure to use visual aids that are clear, concise, and relevant to your message.

Whether you're giving a presentation to a group of colleagues or speaking at a conference, public speaking is an important skill for effective communication.

Practise your public speaking skills by giving presentations, joining a Toastmasters group, or taking a public speaking course.

Use more effective email communication. Email is a common form of communication in both business and personal life. Make sure to use effective email communication by using a clear and concise subject line, using bullet points to organise your thoughts, and proofreading before sending.

Use social media more effectively and utilise several platforms. Social media is a powerful tool for communication, but it's important to use it effectively. Make sure to use appropriate language and tone, respect others' boundaries, and be mindful of the information you share.

Always communicate effectively in meetings which is an important forum for communication, but they can also be time-consuming and unproductive if they're not managed effectively. Make sure to come to meetings prepared, stay on topic, and encourage participation from all members.

Communicating effectively in virtual meetings such as video conferencing and webinars, are becoming more common as technology improves. Make sure to communicate effectively in virtual meetings by using clear audio and video, paying attention to your body language, and being mindful of time zones if you're meeting with people from different parts of the world.

Keep learning and practising your forms of communications. Effective communication is a skill that can be developed and improved over time. Keep learning about different communication techniques and practices, and make an effort to practise these skills in your daily life.

The more you practise, the better you'll become at communicating effectively in both business and personal situations.

In conclusion, effective communication is a critical skill for success in both business and personal life. By practising active listening, communicating clearly and concisely, using nonverbal cues effectively, being aware of your tone, using assertive communication, knowing your audience, using appropriate mediums for communication, emphasising the benefits to your audience, using storytelling, seeking feedback, practising empathy, using positive language, being specific, using inclusive language, using visual aids, practising public speaking, using effective email communication, using social media effectively, communicating effectively in meetings, and communicating effectively in virtual meetings, you can become a more effective communicator and build stronger relationships with others.

Remember to keep learning and practising these skills, as effective communication is a skill that can be developed and improved over time. "Effective communication is a crucial skill that can help us to build stronger relationships, resolve conflicts, and achieve our goals."

The twentieth degree is being a lifelong learner.

"The thirst for knowledge and the desire to learn are key qualities of a lifelong learner."

"Being a lifelong learner means being open to new ideas, perspectives, and ways of thinking." Lifelong learning is not just about acquiring new skills or knowledge, but also about constantly growing and evolving as a person. Lifelong learning is a mindset, not just a set of skills. It involves a willingness to learn and grow throughout our entire lives. Regardless where you are in life, a student, mom or an executive, learning never stops. Whether it is reading an article, a chapter or a whole book the power of knowledge is a powerful skill to master. Success often requires staying curious and eager to learn new things. This means being open to new ideas and approaches, and being willing to learn from others and from your own experiences. We can learn to build our knowledge by implementing these steps in this chapter and applying in our daily lives. We accomplish this by defining your learning goals.Before you can start your journey as a lifelong learner, it's important to identify what you want to learn and why. Consider your personal interests, career goals, and areas where you feel you could benefit from additional knowledge or skills.

Make a list of the subjects or topics you'd like to explore, and try to narrow it down to a few key areas that you can focus on.

Set aside dedicated learning time: To be a successful lifelong learner, you'll need to make time for learning in your schedule. This might mean setting aside a few hours each week for self-study, or making a commitment to learning something new each day. Whatever your schedule allows, it's important to make learning a consistent part of your routine.

One of the key benefits of being a lifelong learner is the opportunity to connect with others who share your interests and passion for learning. Look for local groups or organisations related to your areas of study, or seek out online communities where you can connect with like-minded learners.

Everyone learns differently, so it's important to experiment with different learning styles and approaches to find what works best for you. Some people prefer to learn through reading and writing, while others may prefer hands-on learning or listening to lectures. Try a variety of methods and see what resonates with you. There are countless resources available for lifelong learners, including books, online courses, lectures, and workshops. Make use of these resources to supplement your learning and deepen your understanding of your chosen subjects.

Simply consuming information isn't enough to truly learn and retain new knowledge. To truly learn, it's important to engage with the material and practise what you're learning.

This might involve trying out new concepts or skills, asking questions, or teaching what you've learned to others

As you learn, it's important to track your progress and reflect on what you've learned. This can help you stay motivated and see the progress you're making. Consider keeping a learning journal where you can record your thoughts, questions, and insights.

Mentors and advisors can be invaluable resources for lifelong learners. These are people who have expertise in your areas of study and can offer guidance and support as you learn. Look for opportunities to connect with mentors and advisors, whether through formal programs or informally through your learning community.

Learning isn't always easy, and you'll likely encounter challenges and setbacks along the way. When this happens, it's important to view these experiences as opportunities to learn and grow. Don't be afraid to make mistakes – embrace them as a natural part of the learning process.

Curiosity and an open mind are key qualities of a lifelong learner. Make a habit of asking questions and seeking out new information and perspectives. This will help you stay engaged and motivated to continue learning.

Learning can be mentally and emotionally draining, so it's important to take breaks and recharge regularly. Make sure to give yourself time to rest and recharge so that you can come back to your studies with renewed energy and focus.

While learning is an important part of being a lifelong learner, it's also important to find a balance with other activities and responsibilities. Make sure to set boundaries and prioritise your time so that you can make room for

As a lifelong learner, it's important to stay up to date with the latest developments and research in your field of study. This might involve subscribing to relevant publications, attending conferences or seminars, or following thought leaders on social media.

Learning doesn't always have to come from formal education or structured learning programs. Keep an open mind and be willing to learn from unexpected sources, such as conversations with friends or colleagues, experiences in your personal life, or even media like podcasts or documentaries.

Lifelong learning doesn't have to be limited to personal interests – it can also be applied to your career. Look for opportunities to learn new skills and expand your knowledge base in your current job, or consider seeking out new career opportunities that allow for ongoing learning and development. One of the best ways to continue learning and growing as a person is to take on new challenges and try new things.

Whether it's trying a new hobby or volunteering for a new project at work, stepping out of your comfort zone can lead to new learning opportunities and personal growth.

To truly become a lifelong learner, it's important to make learning a consistent part of your daily routine. This might involve setting aside a specific time each day for self-study, or simply making an effort to seek out new learning opportunities as they arise.

One of the benefits of being a lifelong learner is the opportunity to explore diverse subjects and experiences. Don't be afraid to branch out and try new things – you never know what you might discover.

Learning can be difficult at times, and it's okay to ask for help when you need it. Whether it's seeking out a tutor or mentor, or simply asking a colleague for guidance, don't be afraid to ask for assistance when you need it.

Always stay motivated, learning can be a long-term commitment, and it's important to find ways to stay motivated and engaged. Consider setting small, achievable goals for yourself and celebrate your progress along the way. You might also try finding a learning partner or accountability group to help keep you on track.

Embrace the journey: Becoming a lifelong learner is a journey, not a destination. Embrace the ups and downs, and remember that the learning process is just as important as the end result. Enjoy the journey and have fun along the way!

Becoming a lifelong learner requires a commitment to ongoing learning and personal growth. It involves setting clear learning goals, making time for learning in your schedule, seeking out diverse learning opportunities, and staying motivated and engaged. It also involves being open to new experiences and being willing to take on new challenges.

"Becoming a lifelong learner requires a sense of curiosity, a desire for self-improvement, and a commitment to continuous learning and growth." By embracing the journey of lifelong learning, you can continue to grow and develop as a person and achieve your goals and aspirations.

The twenty-first degree is being confident.

"Confidence is not a trait that you are born with, but a mindset that you can cultivate and nurture over time."

"Confidence is not about being fearless, but about being brave enough to face your fears and embrace them as opportunities for growth." Confidence is not a destination, but a journey. It requires practice and self-reflection, and it will grow as you learn and grow. True confidence comes from within, and it is not something that can be given or taken away by others. Success often requires confidence in your abilities and in your approach. This means believing in yourself and your abilities, and not letting doubt or fear hold you back. When we understand what confidence is and why it matters we can learn and apply it in our lives. Confidence is a feeling of self-assurance and self-esteem. It comes from a belief in one's abilities and qualities. Confidence is important in business and life because it allows you to take risks, make decisions, and pursue your goals with conviction. It can also help you to inspire others and build trust in your relationships. Know your strengths and weaknesses.To become more confident, it's important to know what you're good at and what you need to work on. Take some time to reflect on your skills and experiences, and consider seeking feedback from others.

This will help you to understand your strengths and identify areas where you can improve.

Confidence comes from a sense of direction and purpose. To become more confident, it's important to set clear goals for yourself and create a plan to achieve them. This will give you a sense of direction and help you stay focused on what you want to accomplish.

Taking care of yourself is an important part of building confidence. This includes getting enough sleep, eating a healthy diet, and exercising regularly. It's also important to manage stress and prioritise your mental health.

Everyone makes mistakes, and it's important to learn from them rather than dwelling on them. When you make a mistake, take a moment to reflect on what happened and what you can learn from the experience. This will help you to build resilience and confidence.

Surround yourself with supportive people who are like minded. The people you spend time with can have a big impact on your confidence. Surround yourself with supportive and positive people who believe in you and your abilities. This will help you to feel more confident and motivated.

Seek out new challenges that will improve your confidence. Stepping out of your comfort zone and trying new things can help you to build confidence. Look for opportunities to try new things, whether it's taking on a new project at work or trying a new hobby.

Learn from role models that you inspire. Finding role models who inspire you can be a great way to build confidence. Look for people who have achieved success in their field or who embody the qualities you admire. Learn from their experiences and use them as inspiration for your own journey.

Build your knowledge and skills through resources available to you. Confidence comes from being knowledgeable and skilled in your field. Take the time to learn and develop your skills, whether it's through formal education or on-the-job training. This will give you a sense of accomplishment and help you to feel more confident in your abilities.

Chapter 10: Communicate effectively

Effective communication is an important part of building confidence in business and life. Work on your communication skills by practising active listening, being clear and concise, and using body language effectively.

Dress for success, your impression is your brand. The way you present yourself can have a big impact on your confidence. Take the time to put together a professional wardrobe and consider your personal style. This will help you to feel more confident and prepared for any situation.

Always practise positive thinking like the law of attraction. Your thoughts and beliefs have a powerful influence on your confidence. Practise positive thinking by focusing on the good things in your life and replacing negative thoughts with more positive ones.
Chapter 13: Stand up for yourself

Confidence also means being able to assert yourself and stand up for what you believe in. Practice standing up for yourself in small ways, such as speaking up in a meeting or saying no to unreasonable requests. This will help you to feel more confident in your own convictions.

Take calculated risk. Confidence comes from being willing to take risks and trying new things. To become more confident, it's important to be willing to step out of your comfort zone and try new things, even if they seem intimidating or challenging. This could be anything from starting your own business to taking a public speaking course.

Build a strong support network. Having a strong support network of friends, family, and colleagues can help you to feel more confident and supported. Take the time to cultivate relationships with people you trust and who are willing to support you in your endeavours.

Seek feedback and criticism.Feedback and criticism can be tough to hear, but they can also be valuable tools for growth and improvement. Seek out feedback from trusted sources and be open to hearing what they have to say. This will help you to identify areas for improvement and build confidence in your abilities.

Practice mindfulness and self-awareness.Mindfulness and self-awareness can help you to stay focused, calm, and confident in any situation. Practice mindfulness techniques, such as meditation or deep breathing, to help you stay present and focused. Learn from failure. Failure is an inevitable part of life, and it's important to learn from it rather than dwelling on it. When you experience failure, take a moment to reflect on what happened and what you can learn from the experience. This will help you to build resilience and confidence. Celebrate your achievements. Confidence comes from a sense of accomplishment, so it's important to celebrate your achievements, big and small.

Take the time to reflect on your accomplishments and recognize the hard work and effort that went into them.

This will help you to feel more confident and motivated. Seek out new opportunities. To continue growing and building confidence, it's important to seek out new opportunities for learning and growth. This could be anything from taking on a new project at work to volunteering for a new cause. Practise self-compassion. Self-compassion is the ability to be kind and understanding towards yourself, even when you make mistakes. Practice self-compassion by being kind and understanding towards yourself, and recognizing that everyone makes mistakes and has room for growth and improvement. This will help you to build confidence and resilience. Building confidence in business and life is a journey that requires self-reflection, hard work, and a willingness to take risks and learn from your mistakes. By understanding what confidence is and why it matters, knowing your strengths and weaknesses, setting clear goals, practising self-care, and surrounding yourself with supportive people, you can build the confidence you need to pursue your goals and achieve success. Remember to be kind and understanding towards yourself, and recognize that building confidence is a process that takes time and effort."Confidence is not about believing that you are perfect, but about believing in yourself and your abilities." With persistence and a positive attitude, you can become more confident in business and life.

The twenty-second degree is to be positive.

"Every day is a new opportunity to choose positivity and make a positive impact on the world around you."

"The power of positivity lies in its ability to inspire and motivate. Embrace it and watch your dreams become a reality." A positive mindset is like a garden. It requires constant care and attention, but the beauty it produces is worth the effort. Success often requires a positive attitude and outlook, and it is important to stay optimistic and hopeful even when faced with challenges. This means focusing on the good and not letting negative thoughts or feelings hold you back. Here are ways that helped me be more positive in life and business.

Eliminating negativity in business and life can be a challenging task, but there are several strategies you can try to help reduce negativity and create a more positive environment:

Identify the source of negativity. Try to understand what is causing the negativity, whether it's a specific person, a particular situation, or a negative mindset. This can help you address the root of the problem and find a more effective solution.

Set positive goals. Start by setting positive goals for yourself and your business. This can help give you a sense of purpose and direction, and can help you stay motivated and focused.

Set boundaries. It's important to protect your time and energy by setting limits on the amount of negativity you are willing to tolerate. This can involve setting boundaries with people who bring negativity into your life, or simply taking time to recharge and take care of yourself when you are feeling overwhelmed.

Surround yourself with positive influences. Seek out people and environments that foster positivity and happiness. This can help balance out negativity and provide a supportive network to turn to when you need it.

Practise positive thinking. Negative thoughts can become a habit, but they can also be replaced with more positive ones. Try using affirmations or reframing negative thoughts to focus on the good things in your life.

Practice gratitude. Take a moment each day to think about the things you are grateful for. This can help you stay positive and focused on the good things in your life and business.

Surround yourself with positive people. Seek out positive and supportive people to be around, both in your personal life and in your business. These people can help lift you up and keep you motivated when things get tough.

Stay organised. A cluttered and disorganised environment can lead to stress and negativity. Make an effort to keep your space clean and organised, which can help you stay positive and focused.

Take care of yourself. Make sure you are taking care of your physical, mental, and emotional health. This includes getting enough sleep, eating well, and engaging in activities that bring you joy and relaxation.

Learn from mistakes. Instead of dwelling on mistakes or setbacks, try to learn from them and move on. This can help you stay positive and focused on the future.

Practise positive affirmations that are widely practised in the Law of Attraction. Repeat positive affirmations to yourself regularly, such as "I am worthy and capable," or "I am strong and resilient." This can help you build self-confidence and stay positive.
Focus on the present moment. Try to stay present and focused on the task at hand, rather than worrying about the past or the future. This can help you stay positive and stay on track.

Practice mindfulness. Take a few minutes each day to focus on your breath and be present in the moment. This can help you stay calm and centred, which can contribute to a positive outlook.

Exercise regularly. Regular physical activity can help reduce stress and improve your mood, which can help you stay positive.

Find ways to de-stress. Find activities or hobbies that help you relax and de-stress, such as yoga, meditation, or spending time in nature.

Take breaks. Make sure to take breaks and give yourself time to recharge. This can help you stay positive and avoid burnout.

Find humour in challenging situations. Try to find the silver lining or a bit of humour in challenging situations. This can help you stay positive and keep things in perspective.

Practice forgiveness. Let go of grudges and resentment, and try to practise forgiveness. This can help you move on from negative experiences and stay positive.

Volunteer. Giving back to others can help you feel good about yourself and your place in the world, which can contribute to a positive outlook.

Seek out new experiences. Try new things and step out of your comfort zone. This can help you stay positive and engaged with life.

Surround yourself with beauty. Make an effort to bring beauty into your environment, whether it's through artwork, plants, or other decorations. This can help lift your mood and keep you positive.

Practise positive self-talk. Pay attention to the way you talk to yourself, and try to replace negative self-talk with positive affirmations.

Seek out positive role models. Look for people who embody the positive qualities you admire, and try to learn from them and emulate their example.

Keep learning. Make an effort to continue learning and growing, whether through formal education or personal development. This can help you stay positive and engaged with life.
Practice gratitude. Take a moment each day to reflect on the things you are grateful for. This can help you stay positive and focused on the good things in your life and business.

You can write down a list of things you are grateful for in a journal, or simply take a few minutes to mentally reflect on the things you are thankful for. Practising gratitude can help you appreciate the present moment and keep things in perspective, which can contribute to a positive outlook.

Additionally, you can try incorporating positive habits and behaviours into your daily routine. For example, you can try starting your day with a positive morning ritual, such as meditating, exercising, or writing in a gratitude journal.

You can also try ending your day with a positive evening ritual, such as reflecting on your accomplishments or setting intentions for the next day. By incorporating positive habits and behaviours into your daily routine, you can create a foundation for a positive outlook and mindset.

"A positive attitude is like a superpower, it gives you the strength and resilience to overcome any obstacle." Remember that it takes time and effort to cultivate a positive mindset, but it is worth it for the benefits it can bring to your business and personal life.

The twenty-third degree is being organised.

"The first step towards achieving your goals is getting organised. It allows you to focus on what's important and eliminate distractions."

"A place for everything and everything in its place. This simple philosophy is the key to organisation and success." The benefits of being organised are endless. It saves time, reduces stress, and increases productivity. Organisation is the foundation of success. Without it, everything else crumbles. Success often requires being organised and efficient in your approach. This means staying on top of your tasks and responsibilities, and not letting clutter or disorganisation hold you back. Here are some ways to be more organised and effective in your work and life.

First we have to identify the areas of your life that need organisation. Take inventory of the different areas of your life, such as work, home, personal finances, health, relationships, and leisure. Identify which of these areas are currently disorganised and causing stress or difficulty for you.

Set clear goals for each area of your life. For each area of your life that needs organisation, set specific, achievable goals.

150

Make sure these goals are SMART (specific, measurable, achievable, relevant, and time-bound).

Create a schedule and plan. Create a schedule that allows you to prioritise the tasks and activities that will help you achieve your goals. Break large tasks into smaller, more manageable steps and plan out when you will complete each step.

Work smart and not hard, eliminate distractions and prioritise your time. Identify and eliminate distractions that are hindering your productivity and focus. Prioritise your tasks and activities based on their importance and deadline.

Create systems and effective routines. Develop systems and routines to help you stay organised and on track. This may include creating checklists, using calendars and reminders, and setting aside dedicated time for specific tasks.

Get organised physically. Create an organised physical space that supports your goals and routine. This may involve decluttering, creating storage solutions, and setting up a functional workstation. Get organised digitally. Use technology to your advantage by creating digital systems and tools to help you stay organised. This may include using productivity apps, cloud storage, and digital calendars and to-do lists.

Stay on top of tasks and responsibilities and set aside dedicated time for task management and stay on top of your to-do list. Use tools such as calendars, reminders, and prioritisation techniques to ensure that you are completing tasks in a timely manner.

Keep track of important information and documents. Create a system for storing and organising important documents, such as receipts, bills, contracts, and documents related to your business or personal finances. Use tools such as digital file storage or physical filing systems to keep track of this information.

Manage your finances effectively. Create a budget and track your spending to ensure that you are financially organised and on track to reach your goals. Use tools such as budgeting apps or spreadsheet software to help you stay organised. Streamline your communication and stay organised by streamlining your communication channels and managing your inbox effectively. Use tools such as email filters and rules, and consider using a project management tool to keep track of tasks and collaborate with team members. Stay on top of appointments and meetings. Use a calendar and reminder system to stay on top of appointments and meetings, and make sure to allow enough time to prepare for them. Consider using a scheduling tool to help you manage your schedule and avoid double-booking.

Delegate important tasks and responsibilities. Identify tasks and responsibilities that can be delegated to others, and find ways to do so effectively. This can help free up your time and allow you to focus on more important tasks and goals. Keep track of your progress. Regularly review and assess your progress towards your goals to ensure that you are staying on track. Use tools such as progress reports, calendars, and checklists to help you track your progress. Always stay motivated. Develop strategies and techniques to help you stay motivated and on track, such as setting rewards for achieving goals, finding an accountability partner, or breaking larger goals into smaller, more manageable steps. Seek help when needed. Don't be afraid to seek help when you need it, whether it's from a professional organiser, a coach, or a trusted friend or family member. There are many resources available to help you become more organised and achieve your goals. Practice mindfulness and self-care. Practice mindfulness and self-care to help you stay focused and manage stress. This may include activities such as meditation, exercise, or taking breaks to recharge. Stay flexible and adaptable. Be prepared to adapt and change your approach as needed, as your goals and priorities may evolve over time.Stay open to trying new strategies and techniques to help you stay organised and achieve your goals.

Review and reassess regularly. Regularly review and reassess your organisation systems and techniques to ensure that they are still effective and serving your needs. Make changes as needed and don't be afraid to try new approaches.

Celebrate your successes. Don't forget to celebrate your successes and the progress you have made towards becoming more organised in business and life. This can help you stay motivated and continue to make progress towards your goals. Becoming organised in business and life can bring many benefits such as increased productivity, reduced stress, and better overall quality of life. By setting clear goals, creating systems and routines, eliminating distractions, and staying on top of tasks and responsibilities, you can effectively organise different areas of your life and achieve your goals. It's also important to stay flexible and adaptable, seek help when needed, and celebrate your successes along the way. With dedication and effort, you can become more organised and enjoy the benefits of a more organised life. "The key to a productive and successful life is organisation. It allows you to accomplish more in less time."

I hope these chapters have provided some helpful tips and ideas for becoming more organised in business and life. Good luck on your journey!

The twenty-fourth degree is being a successful leader.

"True leadership is about empowering those around you to reach their full potential."

"A great leader is one who not only leads by example, but also encourages and supports their team to do the same." The mark of a successful leader is the ability to inspire and motivate others to achieve their goals. Successful leaders are those who are willing to take calculated risks and push their team to achieve greatness. Great leaders are those who are able to adapt and lead their team through any challenge that comes their way. Success often requires being able to lead others and inspire them to achieve their goals. This means being able to communicate effectively, set a good example, and motivate others to succeed. Here are some effective ways to develop your leadership skills.

First you have to develop strong communication skills. This includes being able to clearly and effectively convey your ideas and listen actively to others.

Set clear goals and expectations. Successful leaders are able to articulate their vision and the steps needed to achieve it.

Build a strong team. As a leader, it's important to surround yourself with talented and dedicated individuals who can help you achieve your goals.

Foster a positive work culture. A positive work culture can increase productivity, morale, and retention.

Empower your team. Give your team the support and resources they need to succeed, and allow them to take ownership of their work.

Practice transparency. Be open and honest with your team about the direction of the company and any challenges you may be facing.

Lead by example. Set a good example for your team by being punctual, taking initiative, and showing respect for others.

Build trust. Trust is essential for any successful team. Earn the trust of your team by being reliable, honest, and transparent.

Encourage collaboration. Encourage your team to work together and share ideas to foster innovation and creativity.

Take responsibility for your actions. As a leader, it's important to take ownership of your mistakes and learn from them.

Practise continuous learning. Stay up-to-date on industry trends and best practices, and encourage your team to do the same.

Foster innovation. Encourage your team to think outside the box and come up with creative solutions to challenges.

Build strong relationships. Strong relationships with your team, stakeholders, and clients are key to success.

Embrace change. Be open to new ideas and approaches, and be willing to adapt as needed.

Stay organised. Stay on top of tasks and priorities by staying organised and using effective time management techniques.

Delegate effectively. Trust your team to handle tasks and responsibilities, and delegate accordingly.

Foster work-life balance. Encourage your team to maintain a healthy work-life balance to prevent burnout.

Provide constructive feedback. Offer regular feedback to help your team improve and grow.

Recognize and reward achievement. Show appreciation for your team's hard work and accomplishments.

Stay true to your values. Lead with integrity and be true to your values and beliefs. Clearly define your values:

The first step to staying true to your values as a leader is to be clear about what they are. Take the time to reflect on what is most important to you and write it down. This will help you to stay grounded and true to yourself as you navigate your leadership journey.

Communicate your values. Once you have identified your values, make sure to clearly communicate them to your team. This will help them understand your expectations and what is most important to you as a leader.

Practise what you preach. As a leader, it's important to walk the talk and model the behaviour that you expect from your team. This means living your values every day and making sure that your actions align with your words. Stand up for what you believe in. It's important to be willing to speak up and stand up for what you believe in, even if it's not the popular opinion. This demonstrates to your team that you are committed to your values and that you are not afraid to stand up for what you believe in. Seek out opportunities to align with your values. Look for opportunities to align your work and your leadership with your values. This could mean seeking out projects or initiatives that align with your values, or finding ways to make positive change within your organisation.

Seek feedback and support. It can be challenging to stay true to your values as a leader, especially if they are not aligned with those of your organisation or team. Seek out feedback and support from trusted colleagues or mentors to help you stay on track and stay true to your values.

Overall, staying true to your values as a leader requires self-reflection, clear communication, and a commitment to living your values every day. It's not always easy, but it's worth it to be true to yourself and make a positive impact on those around you.

"A great leader is someone who inspires and motivates their team to reach their full potential."

Empathy: A great leader is able to put themselves in the shoes of their team members and understand their needs and concerns. This allows them to create a positive and supportive work environment where everyone feels valued and heard.

Vision: A great leader has a clear vision of where they want to take their team and is able to effectively communicate this vision to others. This helps to inspire and motivate their team to work towards a common goal. Passion: A great leader is passionate about their work and their team. They are enthusiastic and energetic, and this enthusiasm is contagious, inspiring others to be their best selves. Adaptability: A great leader is able to adapt to changing circumstances and lead their team through challenges and obstacles. They are able to think on their feet and come up with creative solutions to problems. Integrity: A great leader is someone who is honest, transparent, and accountable. They lead by example and set the standard for their team to follow. Communication: A great leader is an effective communicator, able to clearly and effectively convey their ideas and expectations to their team. They are also good listeners and open to feedback from others. Decision-making: A great leader is able to make difficult decisions in a timely and decisive manner. They are able to weigh the pros and cons and make the best choice for the team. Collaboration: A great leader is able to build strong and positive relationships with their team and other stakeholders. They are able to work effectively in a team setting and value the contributions of others. Overall, a great leader is someone who is able to inspire and motivate their team to reach their full potential and achieve success. They possess a combination of qualities that allow them to be effective in their role and make a positive impact on those around them. Becoming a successful leader requires a combination of strong communication skills, clear goals and expectations, a positive work culture, and the ability to empower and trust your team. It also involves continuous learning, innovation, strong relationships, adaptability, organisation, effective delegation, empathy, and the recognition and reward of achievement. "Effective leadership is about building trust and fostering a positive team dynamic that allows everyone to thrive." By focusing on these areas and staying true to your values, you can effectively lead and inspire your team to success

The twenty-fifth degree is being a successful team member.

"Effective teamwork requires trust, communication, and a commitment to excellence from every member of the team."

"A strong team is made up of individuals who are willing to take ownership of their responsibilities and work together towards a common goal." Being a successful team member means being willing to put in the hard work and effort to achieve success, both individually and as a team. A winning team is made up of individuals who are willing to put in the work and support each other to achieve success. A great team member is someone who is able to adapt to change, collaborate with others, and find creative solutions to problems. Success often requires being able to work well with others and contribute to the success of a team. This means being able to collaborate, communicate, and support others in their goals.

Understand the team's goals and objectives: It's important to have a clear understanding of what the team is trying to achieve, so you can align your efforts and contribute to the team's success. Communicate effectively:

Good communication is essential for any successful team. Make sure you are clear and concise in your communication, and actively listen to others to understand their perspectives and ideas.

Be reliable: Show up on time, meet deadlines, and follow through on commitments. Your team members need to be able to count on you to do what you say you will do. Be flexible: Teams often encounter unexpected challenges or changes in direction. Being willing to adapt and go with the flow can help the team stay on track and succeed.

Take ownership: Accept responsibility for your work and the success of the team. This means being proactive in identifying and addressing issues, and being willing to put in the extra effort when needed. Be a good problem-solver: Teams rely on their members to come up with creative solutions to challenges and roadblocks. Develop your problem-solving skills and be willing to contribute your ideas to the team. Seek feedback: Ask for feedback from your team members and superiors, and be open to constructive criticism. This will help you understand your strengths and areas for improvement, and allow you to grow and develop as a team member.

Be a good team player: Work well with others and be willing to collaborate. This means being open to different ideas and viewpoints, and being willing to compromise when necessary.
Practice empathy: Show empathy towards your team members and try to understand their perspective. This will help you build strong relationships and create a positive team culture.

Respect others: Treat your team members with respect and dignity, even if you disagree with them. This includes being mindful of your words and actions, and avoiding gossip or negativity.
Contribute to the team's culture: Help create a positive, productive team culture by being an active participant and model for the behaviours you want to see in the team.

Support your team members: Help your team members succeed by offering support and assistance when needed. This could include offering guidance, sharing resources, or simply being a sounding board.

Build trust: Trust is essential for any successful team. Show your team members that they can count on you by being reliable, transparent, and honest.
Learn from your mistakes: Everyone makes mistakes, but it's important to learn from them and use them as opportunities for growth.

Be open to feedback and take ownership of your mistakes, and use them as opportunities to improve and do better in the future.

Seek out new opportunities for growth: Look for ways to improve your skills and knowledge, and be open to new opportunities for growth and development within the team.
Practice self-awareness: Reflect on your own strengths and weaknesses, and be aware of how your actions and words impact others. This will help you become a more effective team member.

Be open to change: Teams and organisations are constantly evolving, and it's important to be open to change and adapt to new situations. Be willing to try new things and embrace new approaches to work.

Practice gratitude: Express gratitude towards your team members and superiors for their contributions and support. This can help build positive relationships and create a more positive team culture.
Prioritise tasks: To be a successful team member, it's important to have a clear understanding of what needs to be done and to prioritise your tasks accordingly.
Set specific, achievable goals for yourself and work towards them.

Seek out opportunities to lead: While being a team player is important, it's also important to take on leadership roles when appropriate and demonstrate your ability to lead. This could involve taking the lead on a project, offering guidance to other team members, or simply stepping up and taking initiative when needed.

By taking on leadership roles, you can showcase your skills and contribute to the team's success in a more meaningful way.

Being a successful team member requires a combination of skills and qualities, including effective communication, reliability, problem-solving, collaboration, and leadership. It's important to understand the team's goals and work towards them, communicate effectively with your team members, be reliable and flexible, and take ownership of your work.

Additionally, it's important to seek feedback, show empathy, respect others, and contribute to the team's culture. By practising self-awareness, setting goals, and seeking out opportunities for growth and leadership, you can continue to improve and contribute to the success of your team.

The twenty-sixth degree is being humble.

"Pride comes before the fall, but humility leads to true success."

"The most inspiring leaders are often the ones who lead with humility and compassion." True humility is being able to admit when you are wrong and being open to change. To be humble is to be open to learning and growth, even from those who may seem beneath you. True greatness is not about being the loudest or the strongest, it's about being humble and serving others. Success often requires being humble and not letting ego or arrogance hold you back. This means being willing to learn from others and admit when you are wrong, and not letting success go to your head.

Recognize your own limitations and imperfections. No one is perfect, and acknowledging this can help you stay humble in business and life.

Practice gratitude. Take time to appreciate what you have and be thankful for the opportunities and resources that have been given to you.

Seek feedback and be open to criticism. Being willing to listen to others and learn from your mistakes can help you grow as a person and a professional.

Don't let success go to your head. It's important to celebrate your achievements, but don't let them make you arrogant or entitled.

Practice humility in your communication. Avoid using "I" too much and try to listen more than you talk.

Show respect to others, regardless of their position or status. Treat everyone with kindness and respect, and avoid talking down to or belittling others.

Don't brag or boast about your accomplishments. Let your actions speak for themselves and let others recognize your achievements on their own.

Be open to learning from others. No matter how much you know or how successful you are, there is always more to learn. Seek out opportunities to learn from those who have different perspectives or experiences.

Practice humility in your leadership style. Lead by example and be willing to admit when you're wrong. Avoid taking credit for the work of others and give credit where credit is due.

Avoid comparing yourself to others. It's natural to want to compare yourself to others, but it's important to focus on your own growth and development instead of trying to outdo others.

Stay humble in your interactions with customers and clients. Remember that they are the reason for your success and treat them with respect and gratitude.

Be open to new ideas and perspectives. Don't be too set in your ways and be willing to consider different viewpoints and approaches.

Don't let ego get in the way of making tough decisions. It's important to make tough decisions in business, but do so with the best interests of the company and its stakeholders in mind, rather than letting ego or personal ambition guide your actions.

Practice humility in your work relationships. Don't let your ego get in the way of teamwork and collaboration.

Give credit where credit is due. Don't take credit for the work of others or try to steal the spotlight. Recognize and acknowledge the contributions of others.
Stay humble in your personal life. Remember that your success in business doesn't define you as a person and avoid letting it change the way you treat others or yourself. Practice humility in your social media presence. Don't let social media feed your ego by constantly sharing about your achievements or posting selfies. Use it to connect with others and share valuable content.

Seek out opportunities to serve others. Helping others can help keep your ego in check and remind you of the importance of humility.

Don't let your ego get in the way of apologising. If you make a mistake, be willing to admit it and apologise. Remember that success is fleeting. Don't let success go to your head and remember that it's important to stay humble and grounded, even in the face of success.

Surround yourself with people who will keep you humble. Seek out mentors and surround yourself with people who will challenge you and help keep your ego in check. Humility is an important quality to cultivate in both your personal and professional life. It can help you maintain a positive attitude, build strong relationships, and stay grounded and focused on what's most important. There are many ways to practise humility, including recognizing your own limitations, practising gratitude, seeking feedback and being open to criticism, and showing respect to others.

"Humility allows us to be more receptive to others and to see the world through a broader perspective." In a world that often values ego and self-promotion, true humility stands out as a rare and valuable quality. By making a conscious effort to cultivate humility in your daily life, you can become a more effective and respected leader and contributor to your community. So, always try to be humble in business and life.

The twenty-seventh degree is being a good listener.

"The most valuable gift you can give someone is your undivided attention."

"The true mark of intelligence is not the ability to speak, but the ability to listen and understand." Listening is a skill that requires effort and practice, but it is crucial in building and maintaining meaningful relationships. Good listeners are open-minded and non-judgmental, creating a safe space for others to share their thoughts and feelings. Success often requires being a good listener and being able to understand and empathise with others. This means being able to truly listen to what others are saying, and not just waiting for your turn to speak. Here are ways to adapt and improve your listening skills.

The importance of being an effective listener. Effective listening is a crucial skill in both personal and professional settings. It allows you to understand and connect with others, build trust and rapport, and make better decisions. The four types of listening skills. There are four types of listening: passive, attentive, active, and empathic. Passive listening is when you are present physically but not mentally engaged. Attentive listening is when you pay attention to the speaker but do not necessarily offer any feedback or response.

Active listening involves both paying attention and actively responding to the speaker, such as by asking questions or paraphrasing. Empathic listening involves not only paying attention and responding, but also attempting to understand the speaker's perspective and emotions.

The barriers to effective listening. There are several barriers to effective listening that can hinder your ability to fully understand and connect with others. These barriers include distractions, prejudices, assumptions, and lack of interest or motivation.

Overcoming distractions.Distractions can come in many forms, such as noise, technology, or your own thoughts. To overcome distractions, try to eliminate as many distractions as possible, focus on the speaker, and use techniques like taking notes or repeating what the speaker said in your head to help stay engaged. Overcoming prejudices and assumptions. It's natural to have biases and make assumptions, but they can interfere with your ability to truly listen and understand others. To overcome prejudices and assumptions, try to be aware of your own biases and make an effort to suspend judgement while listening.

Overcoming Lack of Interest or Motivation. Sometimes, you may find it difficult to listen because you lack interest in the topic or you don't feel motivated to do so.

To overcome this barrier, try to find something that interests you about the topic or find a way to relate it to your own life. You can also try to find ways to motivate yourself, such as setting a goal or finding a reward for listening effectively.

The benefits of active listening. Active listening involves not only paying attention to the speaker, but also actively responding and engaging with them. Some benefits of active listening include building rapport, increasing understanding and clarity, and resolving conflicts. Practising and improving your listening skills is important. Like any skill, effective listening requires practice and dedication. To improve your listening skills, try setting specific goals for yourself, seeking feedback from others, and actively incorporating listening techniques into your daily interactions. With practice, you can become a more effective listener in both your personal and professional life.

How to practise active listening. To practise active listening, try using techniques such as eye contact, nodding, and verbal affirmations like "I see" or "I understand." You can also try paraphrasing what the speaker said to show that you understand and are paying attention. The benefits of empathic listening. Empathic listening involves not only paying attention and responding, but also attempting to understand the speaker's perspective and emotions.

Some benefits of empathic listening include building trust and rapport, resolving conflicts, and improving communication. How to practise empathic listening. To practise empathic listening, try using techniques such as reflecting feelings, asking open-ended questions, and using body language to show that you are listening and caring. You can also try to put yourself in the speaker's shoes and try to understand their perspective and emotions. The role of questions in effective listening. Asking questions is a crucial part of active and empathic listening. It allows you to clarify misunderstandings, seek more information, and show that you are engaged and interested in the conversation. Types of questions to ask when you are actively listing. There are different types of questions that can be useful in different situations. Open-ended questions allow the speaker to expand on their thoughts and feelings, while closed-ended questions can be used to clarify specific points. When and how to use silence. Sometimes, silence can be a powerful tool in effective listening. It allows the speaker to think and process their thoughts, and it can also give you time to reflect on what has been said. However, it's important to use silence in a way that is respectful and not intimidating or dismissive. How to respond to difficult or emotional conversations. Dealing with difficult or emotional conversations can be challenging, but effective listening can help you navigate these situations more effectively.

Some strategies for responding to these types of conversations include using empathic listening, validating the speaker's feelings, and trying to find common ground or solutions. How to listen to virtual conversations. Virtual conversations, such as phone calls or video calls, can present their own challenges to effective listening. To improve your listening skills in these contexts, try to eliminate distractions, pay attention to nonverbal cues, and use techniques like active listening and empathic listening to stay engaged. The role of cultural differences in listening. Cultural differences can impact how people communicate and listen. It's important to be aware of these differences and to be sensitive to them when listening to others. Some strategies for listening across cultural boundaries include being open-minded, asking questions, and using empathic listening to try to understand others' perspectives. The impact of gender and age on listening. Gender and age can also impact how people communicate and listen. It's important to be aware of these differences and to be respectful and open-minded when listening to others. Listening in group settings. Effective listening is also important in group settings, such as meetings or team projects. To improve your listening skills in these contexts, try to eliminate distractions, pay attention to who is speaking and why, and use active and empathic listening to stay engaged and contribute to the conversation.

Listening in negotiations. Effective listening is essential in negotiations, as it allows you to understand the other party's perspective and interests, and to find common ground and solutions. Some strategies for listening in negotiations include using active and empathic listening, asking questions, and staying open-minded.

The role of listening in leadership. Effective listening is a crucial skill for leaders, as it allows them to understand and connect with their team, make better decisions, and resolve conflicts. Some strategies for improving listening skills as a leader include setting aside time to listen, using active and empathic listening, and encouraging open communication within the team.

Practising and improving your listening skills. "Effective communication is not just about speaking, it's about listening and understanding as well." Being a good listener requires putting aside your own biases and opinions, and truly trying to understand the perspective of the speaker.Like any skill, effective listening requires practice and dedication. To improve your listening skills, try setting specific goals for yourself, seeking feedback from others, and actively incorporating listening techniques into your daily interactions. With practice, you can become a more effective listener in both your personal and professional life.

The twenty-eighth degree is being a successful problem-solver.

"The greatest problems often present the greatest opportunities for growth and innovation."

"Effective problem-solving requires clear and logical thinking, as well as the ability to communicate your ideas effectively."Effective problem-solving requires the ability to break down complex issues into smaller, manageable pieces.To be an effective problem-solver, you must be willing to take risks and embrace uncertainty. The most successful problem-solvers are those who are adaptable and able to pivot when faced with new challenges. Success often requires being able to come up with creative solutions to problems. This means being able to think outside the box and not being afraid to try something new.

Define the problem clearly and accurately. Before you can start solving a problem, you need to understand what it is and why it's important. Take the time to identify the root cause of the problem, rather than just addressing the symptoms.

Generate potential solutions. Once you have a clear understanding of the problem, it's time to brainstorm potential solutions.

Try to come up with as many ideas as possible, even if some of them seem far-fetched or unrealistic.

Evaluate the pros and cons of each solution. Once you have a list of potential solutions, take the time to weigh the pros and cons of each one. Consider the impact each solution will have on the business or life situation, as well as any potential risks or downsides.

Choose the best solution. Based on your evaluation of the pros and cons, select the solution that you believe is the best fit for the problem at hand.

Implement the solution. Once you have chosen the solution, it's time to put it into action. This may involve making a plan, assigning tasks, or taking other steps to ensure that the solution is implemented effectively.

Monitor and evaluate the results. Keep track of how the solution is working and whether it is effectively solving the problem. Be open to adjusting or modifying the solution if it is not producing the desired results.

Learn from the experience. Whether the solution was successful or not, take the time to reflect on what you learned from the process of problem-solving. This can help you become more effective at solving future problems.

Practise critical thinking. Effective problem-solving requires the ability to think critically and logically. Practise developing these skills through activities like reading, writing, and participating in discussions or debates.

Keep an open mind. Be open to new ideas and perspectives, even if they differ from your own. This can help you see problems from different angles and come up with more creative solutions. Learn from others. Seek out opportunities to learn from others who have experience solving similar problems. This can include talking to colleagues, participating in training or workshops, or seeking out mentors or advisors. Effective problem-solving requires being able to keep track of all the information and ideas related to the problem. Stay organised by using tools like lists, calendars, and project management software to stay on top of tasks and deadlines.

Stay focused. It's easy to get sidetracked when trying to solve a problem, especially if it is a complex or challenging one. Stay focused by setting clear goals and breaking the problem down into smaller, more manageable tasks. Take breaks. Problem-solving can be mentally exhausting, so be sure to take breaks when needed. Step away from the problem for a bit, take a walk or do something else to clear your head, and then come back to the problem with a fresh perspective.

Seek outside help when needed. Don't be afraid to seek out help when needed, whether that means asking a colleague for their thoughts on the problem or seeking out an expert in the field. Stay positive. Problem-solving can be frustrating at times, but it's important to stay positive and keep a can-do attitude. Remember that every problem presents an opportunity to learn and grow.

Think creatively. Don't be afraid to think outside the box when solving problems. Look for creative or unconventional approaches that might not be immediately obvious.
Stay flexible. Be open to adjusting your approach to problem-solving as needed. Sometimes the best solution to a problem is not the one you initially thought of, and being open to change can help you find more effective solutions. Be patient. Solving problems can take time, and it's important to be patient and persistent. Don't give up too quickly if a solution isn't immediately apparent – keep working at it and you will eventually find a way to solve the problem. Practise active listening. When seeking out the opinions of others, it's important to actively listen and fully understand their perspective. This can help you see the problem from multiple angles and come up with more well-rounded solutions. Stay calm under pressure. Problems often arise when we least expect them, and it's important to stay calm and composed when facing challenges.

Take deep breaths and try to maintain a clear head, even in the midst of a crisis. Continuously improve your problem-solving skills. Problem-solving is an ongoing process, and it's important to constantly work on improving your skills. Seek out new learning opportunities, practice solving different types of problems, and seek feedback from others to help you grow and improve as a problem solver.

Becoming an effective problem solver in business and life requires a combination of skills and mindset. It involves defining the problem clearly, generating potential solutions, evaluating the pros and cons of each option, implementing the best solution, and continuously learning and improving.

"Being an effective problem-solver means being proactive and taking ownership of finding solutions. Effective problem-solving requires a combination of creativity, critical thinking, and persistence." By developing these skills and staying focused, organised, and positive, you can become an effective problem solver and tackle challenges with confidence and determination.

The twenty-ninth degree is being a successful mentor.

"The greatest legacy we can leave is the investment we make in the lives of others."

"The role of a mentor is not to have all the answers, but to help guide others in finding their own solutions." A successful mentor is able to connect with their mentee on a personal level and create a trusting and supportive relationship. A successful mentor is someone who is able to inspire and motivate others to reach their full potential. Being a successful mentor requires not just imparting wisdom, but also being a good listener and understanding the needs of the mentee. Success often requires being able to help others and support them in their goals. This means being able to provide guidance and advice, and being a positive influence on those around you. Here are ways to be a more effective mentor.

Understanding the role of a mentor. A mentor is a guide and advisor who helps individuals develop their skills, knowledge, and capabilities in their personal and professional lives. As a mentor, your role is to provide support, guidance, and encouragement to your mentee as they pursue their goals and navigate challenges. Being a mentor requires a commitment to helping others grow and succeed.

It also requires patience, empathy, and a willingness to listen and offer constructive feedback.

Setting expectations and goals. Before beginning a mentorship relationship, it's important to establish clear expectations and goals. Discuss with your mentee what they hope to accomplish through the mentorship, and work together to set specific, measurable, achievable, relevant, and time-bound (SMART) goals. Setting expectations and goals helps ensure that both parties are on the same page and helps to keep the mentorship on track.

Building a strong relationship with your mentee. A strong mentorship relationship is based on trust, mutual respect, and open communication. To build a strong relationship with your mentee, it's important to be approachable, reliable, and responsive. Make time for regular check-ins with your mentee and encourage them to come to you with any questions or concerns they may have.

Providing support and encouragement. As a mentor, it's important to provide support and encouragement to your mentee as they pursue their goals. This can include offering guidance and advice, helping to develop a plan of action, and providing a listening ear when they need it. By offering support and encouragement, you can help your mentee stay motivated and focused on their goals.

Offering constructive feedback. As a mentor, it's important to offer constructive feedback that helps your mentee grow and improve. When offering feedback, be specific and focus on behaviours or actions that can be changed, rather than criticising the person themselves. It's also important to balance criticism with praise and to offer feedback in a way that is respectful and supportive. Helping your mentee develop skills and knowledge. As a mentor, one of your key roles is to help your mentee develop the skills and knowledge they need to succeed in their personal and professional lives. This can include sharing your own expertise and experience, introducing your mentee to new ideas and concepts, and helping them find resources and opportunities to learn and grow. Encouraging personal and professional growth. A key goal of mentorship is to help individuals grow and develop in their personal and professional lives. As a mentor, it's important to encourage your mentee to take on new challenges and stretch themselves outside of their comfort zone. You can also help your mentee identify areas of weakness and work together to develop a plan to improve in those areas.

Providing professional connections and resources. As a mentor, you likely have a wealth of professional connections and resources that you can share with your mentee.

Introducing your mentee to industry professionals, offering job search assistance, and sharing resources such as articles, books, and online courses can all be valuable ways to help them grow and succeed. Being a role model. As a mentor, you are a role model for your mentee. It's important to set a good example by being professional, reliable, and ethical in all aspects of your work. By being a positive role model, you can inspire your mentee to strive for excellence in their own life and career.

Providing perspective and advice. As a mentor, you can provide valuable perspective and advice to your mentee as they navigate challenges and make important decisions. By sharing your own experiences and lessons learned, you can help your mentee gain a new perspective and make informed decisions. It's important to remember that you are there to offer guidance and support, but ultimately the decisions are up to the mentee.Being a confidential resource. One of the key benefits of mentorship is the opportunity for mentees to have a confidential resource to turn to for support and advice. As a mentor, it's important to maintain confidentiality and respect the trust that your mentee has placed in you. This means keeping any conversations or information shared during the mentorship private and not sharing it with anyone else without the mentee's permission.

Being flexible and adaptable. No two mentorship relationships are exactly the same, and it's important to be flexible and adaptable as a mentor. Be open to adjusting the mentorship based on the needs and goals of your mentee, and be willing to change course if necessary. Remember that the mentorship is a learning and development opportunity for both parties, so be open to learning and growing alongside your mentee. Provide a safe and supportive environment. A key aspect of effective mentorship is providing a safe and supportive environment for your mentee to share their thoughts, ideas, and concerns. This means creating a space where your mentee feels comfortable being open and honest, and where they know they will be listened to and supported. By providing a safe and supportive environment, you can help your mentee feel more confident and open to learning and growth.

Be a good listener. One of the most important skills for a mentor to have is the ability to listen actively and attentively. By really listening to your mentee and paying attention to what they are saying, you can better understand their needs, challenges, and goals. it's also important to show your mentee that you are listening by giving them your full attention, asking clarifying questions, and providing feedback. Managing your own boundaries. As a mentor, it's important to establish clear boundaries and manage your own time and energy in order to be effective.

This means setting limits on the amount of time you are willing to dedicate to the mentorship and being honest with your mentee about what you can and can't commit to. Managing your own boundaries is essential for maintaining a healthy and productive mentorship relationship. Be available and responsive. While it's important to manage your own boundaries, it's also important to be available and responsive to your mentee. Make sure to set aside regular check-in times and be timely in responding to any requests or questions from your mentee. Being available and responsive shows your mentee that you are committed to the mentorship and that you value their growth and development. Be open to learn from your mentee. While the mentorship relationship is primarily focused on the mentee's growth and development, it's also an opportunity for the mentor to learn and grow. Be open to learning from your mentee and to seeing things from their perspective. Remember that mentorship is a two-way street, and you can learn just as much from your mentee as they can from you. Recognizing the end of the mentorship. All mentorship relationships come to an end at some point, whether it's because the mentee has achieved their goals or the relationship has naturally run its course. As a mentor, it's important to recognize when the mentorship has come to an end and to have a plan in place for transitioning out of the relationship. This can include setting a final meeting to reflect on the mentorship and discuss next steps, and offering ongoing support and resources as needed. Always staying in touch. Even after the mentorship has formally ended, it's often valuable to stay in touch with your mentee. By staying in touch, you can continue to offer support and guidance as needed and stay updated on their progress and accomplishments. Staying in touch also helps to maintain the relationship and can be a source of continued learning and growth for both parties. Being a mentor can be a rewarding and fulfilling experience, and it's something that you can continue to do throughout your career. Look for opportunities to mentor others, whether formally through a mentorship program or informally through your personal and professional networks. By being a mentor to others, you can help make a positive impact on their lives and contribute to the growth and development of others. Reflecting on Your Own Growth as a Mentor. Being a mentor is not only about helping others grow and develop, but it's also an opportunity for personal and professional growth for yourself. Reflect on your own journey as a mentor and consider what you have learned and how you have grown through the process. "Mentorship is not just about career development, but also about personal growth and self-discovery." The most effective mentors are those who lead by example and model the behaviours and attitudes they wish to instil in their mentees. Use this reflection to continue to develop your skills and knowledge as a mentor and to be more effective in your role in the future.

The thirtieth degree is being a successful role model.

"The most effective role models are those who are able to inspire and motivate others to be their best selves."

"Effective role models are good listeners and are able to understand and empathise with others." To be an effective role model, you must be willing to take responsibility for your actions and be accountable for your mistakes. Effective role models are able to build and maintain positive relationships with others. Being an effective role model means staying true to your values and principles, even in challenging situations. Success often requires being a good role model and setting a positive example for others to follow. This means being a person of integrity and character, and being someone that others can look up to. Here are ways to help you become a role model that everyone respects. Define what success means to you. Success looks different for everyone, so it's important to define what it means to you personally. This will help you set specific goals and stay motivated to achieve them. Set clear goals and priorities. To be a successful role model, you need to have a clear sense of what you want to accomplish. Determine your priorities and set specific, measurable, achievable, relevant, and time-bound (SMART) goals to help you stay focused and motivated. Practise self-discipline. Successful role models are self-disciplined individuals who are able to resist distractions and focus on their goals. Develop good habits and routines that support your goals and make self-discipline a priority. Take care of your physical and mental health. Your physical and mental well-being are crucial for success. Take care of yourself by getting enough sleep, eating well, and exercising regularly. Make time for activities that nourish your mental health, such as meditation or hobbies. Cultivate a positive attitude. A positive attitude is contagious and can inspire others to strive for success as well. Practice gratitude and focus on the good things in your life, rather than dwelling on negative thoughts. Be resilient and adaptable. Successful role models are able to bounce back from setbacks and failures and learn from them. Cultivate resilience by building a strong support system and learning to reframe negative situations in a more positive light. Be a good communicator. Effective communication is essential for success in any area of life. Practise good listening skills, speak clearly and concisely, and use body language and nonverbal cues to enhance your message. Develop leadership skills. Successful role models are often leaders in their communities or industries. Develop your leadership skills by taking on leadership roles, building trust, and inspiring others to follow your vision.

Embrace learning and growth. Successful role models never stop learning and growing. Stay curious, seek out new experiences and challenges, and be open to feedback and constructive criticism. Practice humility. Successful role models are humble and recognize that they are not always right. Be open to learning from others and be willing to admit when you are wrong. Be accountable and responsible. Successful role models take responsibility for their actions and are accountable for their mistakes. Practice honesty and integrity and make amends when necessary. Practice empathy and compassion. Successful role models are able to put themselves in others' shoes and show understanding and compassion. Cultivate empathy by listening to others and trying to see things from their perspective. Be a good role model for others. Successful role models inspire others to be their best selves by setting a positive example. Practise what you preach and lead by example. Foster positive relationships. Successful role models are able to build and maintain positive relationships with others. Practise good communication skills, show respect, and be a reliable and supportive friend. Be a good listener. Successful role models are good listeners who are able to really hear what others have to say. Practise active listening by giving the speaker your full attention and trying to understand their perspective.

Help others succeed. Successful role models often help others succeed by offering guidance, support, and encouragement. Be a mentor or coach to those who are seeking to achieve their goals.

Give back to your community. Successful role models often recognize the importance of giving back to their communities and use their skills and resources to make a positive impact. Find ways to contribute to your community, whether through volunteering, donating, or advocating for causes you care about.

Practice gratitude. Successful role models recognize and appreciate the good things in their lives. Practice gratitude by keeping a gratitude journal, expressing gratitude to others, and focusing on the positive aspects of your life. Stay true to your values. Successful role models stay true to their values and principles, even in challenging situations. Determine your core values and make sure your actions align with them. Keep a growth mindset. Successful role models are always looking for ways to grow and improve. Cultivate a growth mindset by being open to learning and growth, embracing challenges, and viewing setbacks as opportunities to learn and improve.

Celebrate your successes. Successful role models recognize and celebrate their accomplishments, both big and small.

Take time to reflect on your successes and the progress you have made towards your goals. Share your accomplishments with others and allow yourself to feel proud of your achievements. Being an effective role model requires a combination of personal qualities, skills, and behaviours. It involves setting personal goals and values, developing self-awareness, communicating effectively, building and maintaining positive relationships, leading by example, being a good team player, embracing diversity and inclusion, managing time effectively, adapting to change, staying humble and open to learning, being accountable, being ethical and transparent, showing empathy and compassion, seeking and giving feedback, managing stress and maintaining work-life balance, continuing to learn and grow, giving back to the community, building a positive and supportive work culture, and being a mentor and role model to others.

"Effective role models are able to inspire others to strive for success by sharing their knowledge and experience." The most effective role models are those who are able to adapt and grow, and who encourage and support the growth of others.It also requires a commitment to continually reflect on and improve your role model skills. By embodying these qualities and behaviours, you can be a positive influence and role model in both your professional and personal life.

The thirty-first degree is being a successful Philanthropist.

"True success as a philanthropist comes from the fulfilment and satisfaction of making a positive difference in the world."

"True success is not measured in material wealth, but in the impact we have on the world around us." Being a successful philanthropist means using your resources and influence to make a positive difference in the world. Philanthropy is not just about giving money, but about giving time, energy, and expertise to make a lasting impact. Successful philanthropists are able to identify and address the root causes of social and environmental issues, rather than just addressing symptoms. True success as a philanthropist comes from the fulfilment and satisfaction of making a positive difference in the world. Successful philanthropists are able to inspire and motivate others to join in their efforts to make a positive impact. Being a successful philanthropist requires a combination of compassion, vision, and strategic thinking. Success often requires being a good member of your community and contributing to the greater good. This means being involved in your community and being willing to give back and help others. In this chapter you will learn how to become a more effective philanthropist.

To start with you have to define your values and goals as a philanthropist. What issues or causes are most important to you, and how do you want to make an impact?

Research potential organisations or causes to support. Look for organisations that align with your values and that have a proven track record of making a positive impact.Develop a budget for your philanthropic efforts. Determine how much time and money you can realistically commit to charitable giving, and allocate your resources accordingly. Consider starting a charitable foundation or joining a giving circle. This can help you pool resources and collaborate with other philanthropists to make a bigger impact. Donate wisely. Do your due diligence to ensure that your donations are being used effectively and efficiently. Get involved in the causes you care about. Consider volunteering your time, skills, and expertise to make a difference. Utilise your business resources and connections to make a difference. Consider using your business's resources, such as its products, services, or employee time, to support charitable causes. Use your social media and personal networks to raise awareness and funds for your chosen causes. Host fundraising events or campaigns to support your charitable causes. Encourage your employees and business partners to get involved in charitable efforts.

Consider implementing a corporate social responsibility (CSR) program at your business. This can help you integrate philanthropy into the core operations of your business. Utilise your skills and expertise to make a difference. Consider offering pro bono services or expertise to organisations or causes that align with your values. Stay informed about the issues and causes you care about. Follow news and developments in your chosen fields, and stay up-to-date on the latest research and best practices. Work with your local community to identify and address pressing needs. Consider partnering with local organisations or starting grassroots initiatives to make a difference in your own community. Collaborate with other philanthropists and organisations to amplify your impact. Consider joining or forming partnerships with other philanthropists or organisations to pool resources and expertise.

Educate others about the causes you care about. Share information and resources with your networks to raise awareness and encourage others to get involved.

Be open to learning and adapting your approach. Be willing to listen to feedback and adjust your strategy as needed to maximise your impact. Practice transparency and accountability in your philanthropic efforts. Keep track of your donations and outcomes, and be willing to share this information with others.

Take a long-term view. Look for ways to create sustainable, lasting change, rather than just addressing short-term needs.

Be persistent and consistent in your efforts. Philanthropy is a marathon, not a sprint. Stay committed to your causes and continue to make a difference over the long haul. Celebrate your successes and the impact you are making. Recognize the difference you are making and take time to appreciate and share your achievements with others.

To be an effective and successful philanthropist, it is important to define your values and goals, research potential causes and organisations to support, develop a budget and plan for your giving, and get involved in the causes you care about. Utilise your business resources and connections, host fundraising events and campaigns, and consider implementing a corporate social responsibility program to amplify your impact.

"Successful philanthropists recognize the importance of collaboration and partnerships in creating lasting change." Stay informed about the issues and causes you care about, work with your local community, collaborate with other philanthropists and organisations, and educate others about the issues you care about. Practice transparency and accountability, take a long-term view, and be persistent and consistent in your efforts.

Finally, celebrate your successes and the impact you are making.

The thirty-second degree is being grateful.

"Gratitude is not just a feeling, but a choice. Choose to be grateful, and watch your life transform."

"Gratitude is the open door to abundance. When we express gratitude, we invite more goodness into our lives." The simple act of expressing gratitude has the power to shift our perspective and bring joy to our present moment. Gratitude is a muscle that gets stronger with use. The more we practise gratitude, the easier it becomes to see the good in every situation. Gratitude is the fuel that drives our growth and helps us overcome challenges. When we are grateful, we are able to find strength and resilience within ourselves. Gratitude is a state of being that allows us to connect with the abundance of the universe. When we are grateful, we open ourselves up to receiving all that the world has to offer. Success often requires being grateful for what you have and not taking anything for granted. This means being thankful for the opportunities and experiences that come your way, and not letting success go to your head. In this chapter you will learn how to embrace and implement gratitude no matter where you are in life.

We start by recognizing the value of gratitude in business and life. Gratitude can improve relationships, increase productivity, and enhance overall well-being.

Make a conscious effort to express gratitude on a regular basis. This can be as simple as thanking coworkers or customers for their contributions, or expressing appreciation for the work that you do.

Practice gratitude by keeping a gratitude journal. Each day, write down three things that you are grateful for. This can help you focus on the positive aspects of your life and business.

Take time to reflect on your blessings. Consider the opportunities and resources that you have been given, and how they have helped you achieve success. Practice gratitude by being present in the moment. Instead of dwelling on the past or worrying about the future, focus on the present and appreciate the good things that are happening around you. Focus on the things that you have, rather than what you lack. This can help you appreciate what you have and cultivate a sense of gratitude.

Practice gratitude by helping others. Consider volunteering your time or resources to support a cause that is important to you. This can help you appreciate what you have and feel more connected to others. Cultivate gratitude by being mindful of your thoughts and attitudes. Make an effort to focus on the positive aspects of your life and business, and try to let go of negative thoughts and attitudes.

Practice gratitude by cultivating a positive mindset. This can involve setting goals and working towards them, as well as focusing on the things that you can control and letting go of those that you cannot.

Practice gratitude by being grateful for the challenges and struggles that you face. These challenges can often help you grow and become stronger, and can help you appreciate the good things in your life even more. Practice gratitude by focusing on the present moment. This can involve taking time to appreciate the beauty around you, or simply being mindful of your surroundings. Practice gratitude by being grateful for the people in your life. Take time to appreciate the relationships that you have, and consider how these people have helped you and made a positive impact on your life. Practice gratitude by being thankful for the small things in life. These can include simple pleasures such as a warm cup of coffee or a sunny day.

Practice gratitude by being grateful for the things that you have accomplished. Reflect on your achievements and consider how they have helped you grow and become the person you are today. Practice gratitude by expressing appreciation for the people who have helped you along the way. This can include mentors, friends, and family members who have supported you and provided guidance. Practice gratitude by being thankful for the opportunities that you have been given. Consider how these opportunities have helped you grow and achieve success, and be grateful for the chance to pursue your passions.

Practice gratitude by being grateful for the support and resources that you have. This can include financial resources, access to education, and the support of friends and loved ones.
Practice gratitude by being thankful for the experiences that you have had. These experiences can shape who you are and help you grow as a person, and being grateful for them can help you appreciate all that you have been through.

Practice gratitude by expressing appreciation for the challenges that you have overcome. These challenges can help you grow and become stronger, and being grateful for them can help you appreciate your own resilience and determination.
Practice gratitude by being thankful for the present moment. This can involve taking time to appreciate the beauty around you, or simply being mindful of your surroundings and the good things that are happening in your life.

Practice gratitude by sharing your appreciation with others. This can involve thanking those who have helped you or simply expressing your gratitude to the people in your life. Sharing your gratitude can help you feel more connected to others and can also inspire others to cultivate a sense of gratitude in their own lives. In conclusion, becoming grateful in business and life involves making a conscious effort to recognize and appreciate the good things in your life. This can involve expressing gratitude on a regular basis, practising gratitude through mindfulness and reflection, and sharing your appreciation with others. "Gratitude is the key to unlocking a life filled with joy and abundance. By cultivating gratitude, we open ourselves up to all the abundance the universe has to offer." Gratitude is the foundation of a happy and fulfilled life. When we cultivate a heart of gratitude, we open ourselves up to a world of possibility and abundance. Cultivating gratitude can have numerous benefits, including improving relationships, increasing productivity, and enhancing overall well-being. By making gratitude a part of your daily routine, you can learn to appreciate the present moment and all that you have been given, and find greater happiness and fulfilment in both your business and personal life.

The thirty-third and final degree of success is being happy.

"Happiness in business and life comes from the realisation that we have the power to create our own success."

"True happiness in business and life is found through the pursuit of purpose and passion, not just profit." Happiness in business and life is found in the balance between hard work and leisure. Take time to enjoy the journey, not just the destination. Happiness in business and life is about finding what brings you joy and making it a priority. Happiness in business and life comes from a combination of personal growth, meaningful relationships, and a sense of accomplishment. Happiness in business and life is the result of taking care of yourself and creating a work-life balance that works for you. Happiness in business and life is about being grateful for what you have and finding ways to give back and contribute to the world. Success is not just about achieving your goals and achieving external recognition, but about being happy and fulfilled in your own life. This means being content with what you have, and not letting external factors dictate your happiness. To help you find happiness in everything you pursue in life let's follow these steps in this final chapter.

Let's start with setting clear goals and priorities. Having a clear sense of what you want to achieve can help you focus your energy and efforts on things that are most important to you.

Practice gratitude. Take time each day to think about the things you are grateful for. This can help shift your focus from negative thoughts to positive ones.

Cultivate strong relationships. Surround yourself with supportive, positive people who lift you up and help you feel good about yourself.

Take care of your physical health. Exercise, eat well, and get enough sleep. These habits can improve your overall well-being and contribute to a happier life.

Find meaning and purpose in your work. Seek out work that aligns with your values and passions, and try to find ways to make a positive impact in the world through your job.

Learn to manage stress. Practice stress-reducing techniques like meditation, yoga, or deep breathing to help you cope with the demands of work and life.

Set boundaries. It's important to know your limits and make sure you have time for rest, relaxation, and self-care.

Practice forgiveness. Let go of grudges and resentments that weigh you down. Forgiving others can help you move on and feel happier.Practice forgiveness of self. Be kind and compassionate towards yourself and try to let go of negative self-judgement. Remember that everyone makes mistakes and it's important to learn from them and move forward.

Find ways to stay engaged and curious. Seek out new experiences and learn new things to keep your mind active and engaged.

Practice mindfulness. Pay attention to the present moment and try to live in the here and now rather than dwelling on the past or worrying about the future.

Seek out social support. Surround yourself with people who care about you and are there for you when you need them.

Take breaks and vacations. Taking time off can help you recharge and come back to work feeling refreshed and rejuvenated.
Learn to say no. It's important to set boundaries and prioritise your time and energy. Saying no to things that don't align with your goals or values can help you focus on what's most important to you. Find ways to give back. Helping others can be a rewarding and fulfilling experience that can bring joy and meaning to your life.

Practice self-care. Make time for activities that nourish your body, mind, and spirit, such as exercise, hobbies, or spending time in nature. Learn to manage your finances. Having a financial plan and budget in place can help you feel more in control of your life and reduce stress.

Seek out professional help if needed. If you're struggling with mental health issues, don't be afraid to seek out professional help. A therapist or counsellor can provide support and guidance on how to cope with challenges and improve your well-being.

Practice kindness and compassion. Treating others with kindness and compassion can improve your relationships and help you feel more connected to others. Seek out opportunities for growth and learning. Look for ways to improve your skills and knowledge, whether through formal education or on-the-job training. Find time for fun and leisure.
Make sure you have time for activities that bring you joy and relaxation, such as hobbies or spending time with loved ones.

Becoming happier in business and life involves a combination of setting clear goals and priorities, practising gratitude, cultivating strong relationships, taking care of your physical health, finding meaning and purpose in your work, managing stress, setting boundaries, practising forgiveness, staying engaged and curious, practising mindfulness, seeking out social support, taking breaks and vacations, learning to say no, giving back to others, practising self-care, managing your finances, seeking professional help if needed, practising kindness and compassion, seeking out opportunities for growth and learning, and finding time for fun and leisure.

"Happiness in business and life comes from setting clear goals and taking consistent action towards achieving them." Happiness in business and life is about finding and living your authentic truth, not just chasing external validation or successBy incorporating these strategies into your daily life, you can create a happier and more fulfilling life for yourself.

To be ultimately successful in everything that you do in life, it takes a combination of hard work, determination, and a willingness to constantly learn and improve. Success is not a destination, but a journey that requires ongoing effort and dedication.

One key aspect of success is setting clear goals and having a clear vision of what you want to achieve. It's important to not only have short-term goals, but also long-term goals that align with your values and passions. Having a roadmap to follow helps keep you focused and motivated as you work towards your goals.

In addition to setting goals, it's important to be disciplined and stay focused on the tasks at hand.

Success requires a level of dedication and commitment that may not always be easy, but is necessary to overcome challenges and setbacks. Staying organised and being efficient with your time can also help you make the most of your efforts.

Another important factor in success is the willingness to take risks and step outside of your comfort zone. Success often requires trying new things and stepping out of your comfort zone, even if it means facing uncertainty or failure. It's important to remember that failure is a natural part of the journey to success, and it's through facing and learning from these challenges that we grow and become better versions of ourselves.

Finally, a key component of ultimate success is a willingness to continuously learn and improve.

Successful people never stop learning and are always seeking new opportunities to grow and develop their skills and abilities. This may involve seeking out new experiences, learning from others, or taking on new challenges.

There are several reasons why the book "33 Degrees of Success" can help you be more successful in business and life.

First, the book also teaches some of the concepts of "mu," which is a Japanese term meaning "unseen," "unobserved," or "infinite potential." The idea behind "mu" is that every individual has an unlimited potential to achieve success and reach their goals, no matter what your circumstances may be. This mindset of infinite potential can be incredibly empowering and can help you overcome any challenges or setbacks you may encounter on your journey to success.

Second, the book provides practical strategies and techniques for tapping into your full potential and achieving success. It discusses the importance of setting clear goals, developing a growth mindset, and finding ways to continuously learn and improve. These are all essential skills that are necessary for success in both business and life.

Third, the book offers valuable insights and wisdom from successful individuals who have applied the principles of "mu" in their own lives and achieved great things. By learning from these role models, you can gain valuable insights and inspiration for your own journey to success.

"33 Degrees of Success" can help you be more successful in business and life by providing a mindset of infinite potential and practical strategies for achieving success.

By applying the principles and techniques taught in the book, you can unlock your full potential and achieve your goals.

The book " 33 Degrees of Success" emphasises the importance of taking action and making things happen. Success requires more than just having a positive mindset – it requires taking concrete steps towards your goals and making them a reality. The book encourages readers to be proactive and take control of their lives, rather than waiting for things to happen to them. This proactive approach can be incredibly powerful in helping you achieve success in business and life.

Another key aspect of "33 Degrees of Success" is the concept of resilience and the ability to bounce back from setbacks and challenges. Success is not a straight line, and there will inevitably be times when you encounter roadblocks or face setbacks. The book teaches readers how to embrace these challenges and use them as opportunities for growth and learning, rather than letting them hold them back. This resilience is an essential quality for anyone looking to be successful in business and life.

"33 Degrees of Success" encourages readers to live a balanced and fulfilling life. Success is not just about achieving professional or financial goals – it's also about finding happiness and fulfilment in all areas of your life. The book teaches readers how to prioritise their time and energy in a way that allows them to pursue their passions and lead a fulfilling life. This holistic approach to success can lead to greater happiness and satisfaction in both business and personal endeavours.

The book "33 Degrees of Success" can help you be more successful in business and life by teaching you the mindset of infinite potential, providing practical strategies for achieving success, and encouraging you to take action, be resilient, and live a balanced and fulfilling life. By applying the principles and techniques taught in the book, you can unlock your full potential and achieve your goals.Ultimate success in life requires hard work, discipline, a willingness to take risks and learn, and a clear vision of what you want to achieve. It's a journey that requires ongoing effort and dedication, but with the right mindset and approach, nothing is impossible.

Dedication

In the vast tapestry of life, each thread is woven with experiences, challenges, and triumphs. As I embark on the journey of documenting the lessons learned and insights gained on the path of entrepreneurship and success, it is only fitting to dedicate this book to the pillars of my life – my kids, family, friends, and every soul I have encountered along this remarkable expedition. To my wife and children, you are the living embodiment of my dreams and aspirations. As I pen down the stories of trials and victories, it is my fervent hope that these words will serve as a guiding light for you. May you inherit not just the knowledge within these pages, but also the unwavering determination and resilience that entrepreneurship demands. I dedicate this book to you with the profound belief that it will inspire you to chase your own dreams, armed with the wisdom passed down from one generation to another. To my family, you have been the bedrock of support, providing strength during turbulent times and celebrating every achievement. This book is a tribute to your unwavering belief in my potential, and the sacrifices you made to foster an environment where dreams could flourish. Your encouragement has been the wind beneath my wings, propelling me to reach heights I once deemed unattainable.

To my friends, the journey of entrepreneurship is a roller coaster, and your camaraderie has been the source of solace and joy. Through the highs and lows, your friendship has been a constant reminder that success is not just about individual accomplishments but the shared joy of collective achievement. This book is dedicated to the laughter we've shared, the late-night conversations that fueled inspiration, and the bonds that have stood the test of time. To everyone I have encountered throughout the years, whether briefly or in profound moments, this book is an acknowledgment of the shared human experience. It is a testament to the belief that success is not a solitary pursuit but a collective endeavour. In dedicating these pages to you, I express gratitude for the lessons learned, the perspectives gained, and the richness added to the tapestry of my life by our interactions.

As I share the principles and anecdotes from my entrepreneurial journey, it is my sincere desire that this book resonates with the dreamers, the doers, and the believers. May it ignite the spark of possibility within every reader and serve as a compass guiding them towards their own definitions of success. In dedicating this book to my kids, family, friends, and every individual who has played a role in shaping my narrative, I extend my deepest gratitude. May the stories within these pages be a source of inspiration and empowerment for generations to come, as we continue to weave the fabric of our dreams, one thread at a time. I hope my book will help you on your journey to success and make your skills more effective in life. @ **Arlind Sadiku**
Entrepreneur & Author "*33 Degrees of Success*"

Instagram: https://www.instagram.com/arlindsadikux/
Facebook: https://www.facebook.com/arlindsadikux
Twitter: https://twitter.com/ArlindSadikux
LinkedIn: https://www.linkedin.com/in/arlindsnetwork/

www.ingramcontent.com/pod-product-compliance
Lightning Source LLC
Chambersburg PA
CBHW030436290526
45786CB00001B/316